Psalms for Recovery

Psalms for Recovery

MEDITATIONS FOR STRENGTH AND HOPE

Barbara Stephens

HarperSanFrancisco
A Division of HarperCollins*Publishers*

FIRST EDITION

Library of Congress Cataloging-in-Publication Data

Stephens, Barbara.
    Psalms for recovery : meditations for strength and hope / Barbara Stephens. — 1st ed.
      p. cm.
   ISBN 0–06–067592–6 (alk. paper)
   1. Twelve-step programs—Religious aspects—Christianity—Meditations.   I. Title.
BV4409.2.S74   1991
242'.4—dc20   90–55314
                                         CIP

---

93 94 95 96 97 BANWI 12 11 10 9 8 7 6 5 4

This edition is printed on acid-free paper that meets the American National Standards Institute Z39.48 Standard.

Introduction

Recovery is a simple, uncomplicated word. There's nothing frightening about just saying it or seeing it, but to experience recovery may evoke every emotion known to humankind, especially at the beginning of the journey.

No matter from what you may be recovering, be it alcohol, drugs, food, sex, gambling, smoking, or relationships, you may have a certain amount of fear and anxiety because you are changing your entire life-style.

Recovery begins when the pain of remaining addicted/codependent has become greater than the fear and pain of change. A child may experience a toothache but refuses to tell anyone because of his or her fear of the dentist. Until the pain of that toothache becomes greater than this fear, the child will continue to suffer. As the pain continues to intensify, the dentist begins to sound better and better. When our addiction/codependency begins to cause more pain than it relieves, recovery begins to look like a possible solution.

The Twelve Steps*

1. We admitted we were powerless over [addiction], that our lives had become unmanageable.
2. Came to believe that a Power greater than ourselves could restore us to sanity.
3. Made a decision to turn our will and our lives over to the care of God *as we understood Him*.
4. Made a searching and fearless moral inventory of ourselves.
5. Admitted to God, to ourselves, and to another human being the exact nature of our wrongs.
6. Were entirely ready to have God remove all these defects of character.
7. Humbly asked Him to remove our shortcomings.
8. Made a list of all persons we had harmed, and became willing to make amends to them all.
9. Made direct amends to such people whenever possible, except when to do so would injure them or others.
10. Continued to take personal inventory and when we were wrong promptly admitted it.
11. Sought through prayer and meditation to improve our conscious contact with God *as we understood Him*, praying only for the knowledge of His will for us and the power to carry that out.

12. Having had a spiritual awakening as the result of these steps, we tried to carry these messages [to others], and to practice these principles in all our affairs.

This book is a daily source of strength for the recovering person. It uses the Twelve Steps and combines them with the Book of Psalms to bring hope, strength, and correction.

This began as my own personal journal of recovery in October 1988. I had been without my "drug of choice" (relationships) for eleven days, and I was in the most emotional turmoil I had ever known. Turning to the Psalms and seeing the Twelve Steps so plainly in many of them encouraged me. I share with you what was a gift to me on one of the most difficult and yet rewarding journeys I've experienced.

B. S.

Psalm
1

*Blessed is the man who does not walk in the
counsel of the wicked. (v. 1)*

Our addictive/codependent thinking is wicked because it is not in our best interest. Sometimes friends and relatives who are not recovering or do not understand the Twelve-Step program may give counsel that is unhelpful or unwise. Therefore, we need to look to God for our direction, for our counsel. As we draw strength from him and from his Word, we will become stronger and experience victory. Our support groups are another source of understanding, love, and helpful counsel, and we are able to stand strong as we listen with an open heart to others' stories of recovery.

Still another source of wise direction is our sponsor. All of these people make up a network of comfort, encouragement, and inspiration. So we do not have to turn to the counsel of those who do not understand.

*Lord, help me to use wisely the tools
of recovery.*

Psalm
2

Blessed are all who take refuge in him.
  (v. 12)

Probably at no other time in our lives will we be quite as vulnerable as we are during the first stage of our recovery. Probably at no other time in our lives will our pain be any greater. What a comfort to realize that at these times we can take refuge in him. When our emotions are in a million pieces, we can take refuge in his Word. When there is no other, he is there—day after day after day. When we are most vulnerable, we can run to the safety of our Father. When we are hurting, we can run into the strong tower of his acceptance. He is our refuge, and with him we can make it.

Father, teach me that at my most vulnerable
times, I can run to you.

Psalm
3

*O Lord, how many are my foes! How many
rise up against me!*
*Many are saying of me, "God will not deli-
ver him."*
*But you are a shield around me, O Lord; you
bestow glory on me and lift up my head.*
*To the Lord I cry aloud, and he answers me
from his holy hill. . . .*
*From the Lord comes deliverance. May your
blessing be on your people. (vv. 1–4; 8)*

Many a day we have felt this in our recovery. Our
addiction/codependency is too big to be conquered. But God isn't hampered by what we
feel—his promise doesn't hinge on what we feel.
When he says he'll do something, he does it.

We find Step Two in verse 8 of this psalm: We
came to believe that God could restore us to sane
living. God and our cooperation with his plan to
deliver us are sure to produce health and victory.

*Lord, help me to realize that feelings are
temporary.*

Psalm
4

Answer me when I call to you, O my righteous
God. Give me relief from my distress; be
merciful to me and hear my prayer.
How long, O men, will you turn my glory into
shame? How long will you love delusions and
seek false gods?
Know that the Lord has set apart the godly
for himself; the Lord will hear when I call
to him.
In your anger do not sin; when you are on your
beds, search your hearts and be silent.
Offer right sacrifices and trust in the Lord.
Many are asking, "Who can show us any
good?"
Let the light of your face shine upon us, O
Lord.
You have filled my heart with greater joy than
when their grain and new wine abound.
I will lie down and sleep in peace, for you
alone, O Lord, make me dwell in safety.
(vv. 1–8)

Whether emotionally dependent or addicted we are in such distress that we call out to God. At one time, the drug or person may have eased our pain, but now there is no relief. Still in denial, we continue to hold the illusion that maybe once more the pain can be eased by returning to the addiction. Hitting bottom brings us to the truth that we must turn our lives and wills over to God. The outcome is that God can and will fill the depths within with joy and contentment. No drug or relationship could ever do that for us on a permanent basis.

Father, in my distress, give me courage to follow your direction.

Psalm
5

The Prayer of the Recovering Person

*Give ear to my words, O Lord, consider my
sighing.*
*Listen to my cry for help, my King and my
God, for to you I pray.*
*In the morning, O Lord, you hear my voice; in
the morning I lay my requests before you and
wait in expectation.*
*You are not a God who takes pleasure in evil;
with you the wicked cannot dwell.*
*The arrogant cannot stand in your presence;
you hate all who do wrong. . . .*
*But I, by your great mercy, will come into your
house; in reverence will I bow down. . . .*
*Lead me, O Lord, in your righteousness because
of my enemies—make straight your way
before me.*
Not a word from their mouth can be trusted.
*For surely, O Lord, you bless the righteous; you
surround them with your favor as with a
shield. (vv. 1–5; 7–9; 12)*

This psalm may sound vaguely familiar to the recovering person comparable to prayers cried out to God in the midst of discouragement. Many times we lay out an agenda for God to meet and when it does not happen as we planned, we lose heart. But the secret of peace is to wait for God to give us our agenda and then to have a heart full of expectancy. Prayer is another way of taking refuge on those tough days, and taking refuge produces gladness and a song in our hearts. We love his name, rejoice, and are blessed because we are protected by his favor.

In Step Two on our journey of recovery, he places a shield about us that will assure our victory.

Father, remind me that soon I will be glad and I will sing again.

Psalm
6

O Lord, do not rebuke me in your anger or
discipline me in your wrath.
Be merciful to me, Lord, for I am faint; O Lord,
heal me, for my bones are in agony.
My soul is in anguish. How long, O Lord, how
long?
Turn, O Lord, and deliver me; save me because
of your unfailing love. (vv. 1–4)

Recovering from our addiction/codependency
brings us in touch with feelings that overwhelm
us. It is difficult for us to understand that God
isn't out to "get us."

- We fear God's anger.
- We need his mercy.
- We are weak.
- We need his healing.
- We feel he has left us.
- We need deliverance.

After being "sober" several days, we can begin
to *feel* again. Our feelings say we're being pun-
ished—we are faint; we are weary; we need the
God of the second Step to restore us.

Our hearts and souls are in such pain. How
long will we suffer? (Remember the child with the
toothache.)

God's unfailing love will deliver us.

Our symptoms are so painful that we weep; we cry. After we cry so much, our eyes are blurred. We are in sorrow because of our addiction.

We are entirely ready to have God remove all these defects, as in Step Six.

We will be free.

Father, remind me often that I will enjoy a life of freedom once more.

Psalm
7

O Lord my God, I take refuge in you; save and
*   deliver me from all who pursue me [my*
*   addiction/codependence],*
or they will tear me like a lion and rip me to
*   pieces with no one to rescue me. (vv. 1–2)*

Until there is a rescuer, we keep on in our addictive/codependent life-styles. We must experience the consequences fully before we will truly recover. Until then, we continue self-defeating thinking and behaving. When we have "bottomed out," we will turn our lives and wills over to God as we understand him.

Addiction/codependency is like a lion and shows absolutely no mercy as it rips and tears our lives apart. Dare we not continue on this journey into recovery?

Lord, give me strength to continue the
journey—even on difficult days.

Psalm
8

When I consider your heavens, the work of your
  fingers, the moon and the stars, which you
  have set in place,
what is man that you are mindful of him, the
  son of man that you care for him?
You made him a little lower than the heavenly
  beings and crowned him with glory and
  honor.
You made him ruler over the works of your
  hands; you put everything under his feet.
  (vv. 3–6)

We can trust our lives in the care of God. We can
depend on him for whatever we need. When we
consider all that he has made and done, it is baf-
fling to realize that we are important to him.

God, our Father, has ordained great things for
each of his children, but until we are able to reach
out of our addiction/codependency we will never
experience those things. It's amazing that he gives
us dominion, ability to rule over the works of his
hands, but we are powerless over our addiction.
That powerlessness puts us in a position for a
great and mighty God to take charge of our lives
and bring us along in our journeys of recovery.

Father, thank you for loving me into recovery
with "tough love."

Psalm
9

My enemies turn back, they stumble and perish
  before you. . . .
The Lord is a refuge for the oppressed, a
  stronghold in times of trouble.
Those who know your name will trust in you,
  for you, Lord, have never forsaken those who
  seek you. . . .
For he who avenges blood remembers; he does
  not ignore the cry of the afflicted.
  (vv. 3; 9–10; 12)

Because God is working with us in our recovery,
we want to praise him and tell others, as in Step
Twelve. Our addictions gradually lose their tight
hold on our lives. Many different emotions and
pains may have encouraged our addictions. As
God heals and we work with him, even the memory of them is healed. We can turn them over to
him. We can hide in him. God will not abandon
us. God will not ignore us when we turn to him,
even when our addictions scream. In our great
need, we can turn to him; even in our affliction,
we can hope. He is able.

Father, you are able especially when I
  am powerless.

Psalm
10

Why, O Lord, do you stand far off? Why do
you hide yourself in times of trouble? . . .
His victims are crushed, they collapse; they fall
under his strength. (vv. 1; 10)

On those days when our addiction is screaming,
we may feel that God stands far away, that he
hides from us when we are in trouble.

Many times the enemy (the addicted self)
craves, in our hearts and souls, for the relief we
once knew. When we're really into addiction, we
don't seek God—our minds are so caught up in
"stuff" that there is no room for thoughts of God.

But somewhere deep inside of us a part has begun to recover, and God keeps reminding us that
he isn't absent, even when we can't feel him.

Father, give me strength to endure this
temporary craving.

Psalm
11

The Lord is in his holy temple; the Lord is on
his heavenly throne. He observes the sons of
men; his eyes examine them.
The Lord examines the righteous, but the wicked
and those who love violence his soul
hates. . . .
For the Lord is righteous, he loves justice;
upright men will see his face. (vv. 4–5; 7)

At Step Six, we were entirely ready to have God
remove all these defects. Our only hope now is to
learn how to do this.

In the midst of our pain, we take refuge in the
Lord. Our wounded souls constantly pull and beg
and long. "Stinking thinking" shoots from the
darkness within us, trying to gain control.

God doesn't abandon us in our struggle. He
sees us, knows us, and is moved by compassion
for what we feel.

Because of what our addiction/codependence
does to us, he hates it. He will purge from our
beings the very wound or root that has caused us
to seek the drug of choice, be it people, drugs,
alcohol, sex, gambling, success, food, or nicotine.

The Lord is righteous; he loves justice and truth. As we are able to see that he is not mad at us but at the addiction that has nearly destroyed our lives, we are able to admit our problem with honesty, openess, and willingness.

Addiction stole our joy, our happiness, our lives, and even our wills—but God restores back to us all that was lost.

Lord, teach me to be honest with myself, open to you, and willing to risk with others.

Psalm
12

*O Lord, you will keep us safe and protect us
from such people forever. (v. 7)*

God cares that we are struggling with recovery.
He cares that at times the addictive personality
almost gains control, and he protects us from
those who would pull us back.

God will keep us safe; he will protect us from
the pull of our addiction/codependency. Our willingness to follow when and where he leads, to
wait when he isn't moving, and to obey when he
speaks assures us of another day of recovery.

*Lord, teach me when to wait and when
to follow.*

Psalm
13

How long, O Lord? Will you forget me forever?
How long will you hide your face from me?
How long must I wrestle with my thoughts and
every day have sorrow in my heart? How
long will my enemy triumph over me?
Look on me and answer, O Lord my God. Give
light to my eyes, or I will sleep in death; my
enemy will say, "I have overcome him," and
my foes will rejoice when I fall.
But I trust in your unfailing love; my heart
rejoices in your salvation.
I will sing to the Lord, for he has been good to
me. (vv. 1–6)

Emotionally this is the way it feels:

- God has forgotten us (v. 1).
- God is hiding his face.
- We wrestle with our thoughts (v. 2).
- Every day we have sorrow in our hearts.
- How long will our enemy triumph over us?
- We need to hear from God (v. 3).
- We need insight before we crack emotionally.
- The enemy is laughing (v. 4).
- We *must* trust his unfailing love (v. 5).
- We will sing again because he has been good to us (v. 6).

Lord, teach me the secret of one day at a time.

Psalm
14

The fool says in his heart, "There is no God."
They are corrupt, their deeds are vile; there is
no one who does good.
The Lord looks down from heaven on the sons of
men to see if there are any who understand,
any who seek God.
All have turned aside, they have together
become corrupt; there is no one who does
good, not even one.
Will evildoers never learn—those who devour
my people as men eat bread and who do not
call on the Lord?
There they are, overwhelmed with dread, for
God is present in the company of the
righteous.
You evildoers frustrate the plans of the poor, but
the Lord is their refuge. (vv. 1–6)

Step Two tells us we came to believe that a Power
greater than ourselves could restore us to sanity.
Maybe another word for insanity would be *fool*.
When we live with the belief that we can do our
own thing—or run our lives—our whole lives are
a mess. Our deeds are vile, and we find it impossible to do good.

For many addicts, this is a very hard lesson to learn. But until we come to the awareness that God is and that he can restore us to sanity, we will flounder and fall. Stability is the result of acknowledging God as the source of our recovery.

O God, remind me that I'm not big enough
without you.

Psalm
15

Lord, who may dwell in your sanctuary? Who
may live on your holy hill?
He whose walk is blameless and who does
what is righteous, who speaks the truth
from his heart and has no slander on his
tongue, who does his neighbor no wrong
and casts no slur on his fellow man, who
despises a vile man but honors those who
fear the Lord,
who keeps his oath
even when it hurts, who lends his money
without usury and does not accept a bribe
against the innocent.
He who does these things will never be
shaken. (vv. 1–5)

It is one thing to know *about* God; it is quite another to *know* him. Prayer and meditation upon
his Word help us get to know him.

And yet, Lord, even when we do our best to
get to know you, sometimes our own fears and
wrong beliefs interfere. We want to come close to
your sanctuary. We desire to live on your holy
hill. But our own thoughts tell us that, because of
the mess we've made of our lives, you would not
want us anywhere near you. Lord, in our sane
moments we know that isn't true. Teach us how
to know you and how to really trust you.

In recovery, we are learning how to live with other less-than-perfect people, and we are learning how to speak our feelings without crushing someone else. Becoming trustworthy is often a difficult task because of our past record, and yet that is such an important part of recovery. So we will endure the doubts that others have about us; one day we will be beyond this. Today we are willing.

Father, draw my recovering heart closer to you through meditation and prayer.

Psalm
16

Keep me safe, O God, for in you I take refuge.
I said to the Lord, "You are my Lord; apart
from you I have no good thing." (vv. 1–2)

Those who were so addicted/codependent may
find it strange to realize that apart from the Lord
we have nothing good. Left to our own devices,
we will destroy everything good that comes our
way. But we are very aware that success in recovery requires a partnership. God plus the one recovering person, daily walking out the stages of
recovery, will surely bring victory. We can't do it
without God, and he doesn't need recovery. So
it's a twosome.

As long as we keep the Lord active in our recovery and hold onto him, we will not be shaken.
But when we think we can do it alone, watch out!

Some days our hearts are so glad that recovery
is now our life-style, and we rejoice. Our bodies
begin to relax and rest securely because we are
confident that God will not abandon us to the
grave.

As recovery progresses, our lives are filled with
joy because we begin to *really enjoy* being in his
presence. Today we take refuge in the Lord.

Lord, give me constant awareness that recovery
is partnership.

Psalm
17

Though you probe my heart and examine me at night, though you test me, you will find nothing. I have resolved that my mouth will not sin. (v. 3)

Step Ten reminds us to continue to take a personal inventory and, when we are wrong, to promptly admit it. We must allow God to probe the depths of our heart and examine us. So often we are able to rationalize our behavior and thinking, and we excuse ourselves. So in recovery, we must be willing to expose ourselves to God even when we think we're coming along OK. Growth only comes as we open ourselves up to him, knowing that he will not reject even the worst about us. When we realize that all of our personal self-help, self-improvement efforts have not truly changed us, *then* we are more willing to allow him to test us.

What a comfort to feel that God looks at us, even in recovery, even on not-so-good days, as the apple of his eye and that he hides us in the shadow of his wings when the addiction/codependency is pulling at our very hearts.

Our mortal enemy is our disease of addiction/codependency. Addiction/codependency is concerned about only one thing—to take over, control, defeat, and destroy. God *will* restore us to sanity.

Father, admitting I am wrong is so hard—give me strength to do it.

Psalm
18

I love you, O Lord, my strength. The Lord is
my rock, my fortress and my deliverer; my
God is my rock, in whom I take refuge. He
is my shield and the horn of my salvation,
my stronghold.
I call to the Lord, who is worthy of praise, and
I am saved from my enemies. (vv. 1–3)

Some days of recovery are just bad days. Pain
overwhelms us, and our hurt and grief scream.
On those days it would be so easy to slip, to go
back to the old ways.

But on those days when we are too weak, he is
our strength. When we are shaky, he is our rock.
When we need security, he is our fortress. When
we need a safe place, he is our refuge. And wonder of wonders, he is committed to our recovery.
Even on those days when we know for sure we'll
never make it, he stands firm.

Just think: God, our Father, the Creator of this
universe, is interested in our recovery. Only he
can keep our lamp burning, and he does turn our
darkness into light.

God, on bad days hold on tightly to me.

Psalm
19

The heavens declare the glory of God; the skies
proclaim the work of his hands.
Day after day they pour forth speech; night
after night they display knowledge. . . .
May the words of my mouth and the meditation
of my heart be pleasing in your
sight. . . . (vv. 1–2; 14)

In recovery, it is easy to get so caught up in programs, sponsors, and meetings that we forget to
improve our conscious contact with God. This is
a serious downfall and can lead to relapse if we
are not cautious. This psalm tells us a good way
to improve conscious contact—through nature.
Take time to enjoy God's love gift of Creation.
Walk in the woods; listen to the water rushing in
a stream; look at the stars and moon; smell the
flowers. Slow down and take time to hear what
nature tells us about God. Drive through the
country, in the mountains, or take some scenic
route and enjoy the voice of nature. Watch for
sunsets and sunrises and beautiful cloud forma-
tions, and on rainy days, look for those beautiful
rainbows. Watch the birds and animals, and enjoy
the beautiful world our Father created for us.

On busy days, Lord, speak to me in ways that I
will hear.

Psalm
20

*May the Lord answer you when you are in
     distress; may the name of the God of Jacob
     protect you.
May he send you help from the sanctuary and
     grant you support from Zion.
May he remember all your sacrifices and accept
     your burnt offerings.
May he give you the desire of your heart and
     make all your plans succeed.
We will shout for joy when you are victorious
     and will lift up our banners in the name of
     our God. May the Lord grant all your
     requests. (vv. 1–5)*

Just as Step One is important, so is Step Twelve.
It is the continuing of the recovery process, and
this psalm is a prayer for others in recovery. Our
aim should be to constantly hold up in prayer
those who are struggling with recovery. May our
prayer be that God will answer those in distress.
May he protect those who are struggling. May he
send help and grant support. May he remember
the sacrifices, give the desires of the heart, and
make his plans succeed. May he grant the requests according to his will.

Together we will shout for joy when we are victorious, and we will proclaim to other addicts/codependents that recovery is a real possibility for those who turn to him.

God, use me to reach out to others struggling with recovery.

Psalm
21

*O Lord, the king rejoices in your strength. How
great is his joy in the victories you give!
(v. 1)*

Think of the "king" in this psalm as ourselves.
When we finally do learn how to "turn it over,"
we can learn to rejoice in his strength. He gives
victory, and we begin to have joy as we take each
step out of addiction, out of the sickness, out of
the pain. When the desire of the heart is recovery—wholeness—he begins work to that end. No
matter what a mess our lives may have been in,
God welcomes us to come as we are. He pours
out rich blessings even though we are so sick and
messed up at the time; he pours blessings on us
even when we do not realize it. God gives us life
when we have been consumed with death. God
grants us victories each day, one step at a time.
Each sober minute is a victory.

When we trust in the Lord and realize his unfailing love, we will not be shaken for long. God
will give us strength, courage, and power to live
sober lives.

Our addictive nature is always setting us up to
fall, but God sets us up to be winners.

*O Lord, grant that I may follow your pathway
to victory.*

Psalm
22

My God, my God, why have you forsaken me?
Why are you so far from saving me, so far
from the words of my groaning?
O my God, I cry out by day, but you do not
answer, by night, and am not silent.
(vv. 1–2)

Although this is a prophecy about Jesus and his Crucifixion, it is also the cry of the suffering one's heart.

The desperate cry of "My God, why have you forsaken me?" is the actual feeling we have from time to time. In our pain, it seems that surely God has abandoned us.

Many times it seems that God is not listening and that he is not doing anything to help us. We have seen with our eyes the deliverance of others from a life-style of addiction; we have heard their stories. God delivered them—they are walking in recovery. So what is wrong with us? Our own thoughts mock us, telling us that we are foolish to trust in the Lord to rescue and deliver us.

Yet God delivered us from our mother's womb; he taught us that we can trust; he has been faithful from our conception. He will not let us be defeated now. Our emotions tell us he is absent; trouble seems much closer than he does, and yet no one else can really help.

Addiction seems to have the power of a bull, especially at the beginning of our recovery. The pull of our emotions and the physical pain seem like lions tearing their prey. Even our bones cry out in pain.

Realizing that only God can help us at this point, we can reach out to him, even when our emotions tell us that he is far away.

We want recovery to produce instant happiness, but recovery is "here a little, there a little,". . . day by day.

Lord, remind me that all of life is "here a little, there a little."

Psalm
23

The Lord is my shepherd, I shall not be in want. (v. 1)

Actually, only God can fill the longing that previously we tried to drown in our addiction/codependency. Yet we often think we need *someone who is touchable*, someone who can "fix" our pain. When we are caught up in the fantasy, we begin to seek the "someone." Until we come to grips with the knowledge that no person can reach the depths of us or stop the pain and longing, we will not recover. The fantasy must die so that we can once and for all reach out to the *only* One who can face the longing with us.

Even though the pain is at times more than we think we can bear—even when the pain screams that God is absent—he is still present. He is with us, even when we are sure he is not. After all, he promised.

As we learn to face the loneliness and longing with him, needs that have driven us are eased and finally met, and we are free to take further steps in recovery.

Day by day or minute by minute we come to realize that he is able and willing to meet the needs of our hearts so that we actually lack nothing.

Father, fill my empty longing with yourself and your love.

Psalm
24

*Who may ascend the hill of the Lord? Who may
   stand in his holy place?
He who has clean hands and a pure heart, who
   does not lift up his soul to an idol or swear
   by what is false. (vv. 3–4)*

Coming to know God is a very important step in
recovery. Much of what we know from our past is
clouded by misinformation and must be replaced
by accurate facts. God is so powerful. He created
the world; surely he can handle our lives, our re-
coveries. He can be trusted to take us from the
lowest pit of addiction to the heights of recovery—but only as we allow him to lead us, only as
we are willing to follow.

Progressive recovery frees us from the idol of
addiction/codependency. But we have to remind
ourselves that recovery is progressive and we cannot progress unless we are willing to take those
daily steps.

*Father, help me take steps when sitting would
be easier.*

Psalm
25

To you, O Lord, I lift up my soul; in you I
trust, O my God.
Do not let me be put to shame, nor let my
enemies triumph over me.
No one whose hope is in you will ever be put to
shame. . . .
Remember not the sins of my youth and my
rebellious ways; according to your love
remember me, for you are good, O Lord.
(vv. 1–3; 7)

This is the prayer of the recovering: "I lift up my soul" (but only after our souls become so troubled and diseased).

When we were in so much emotional pain, we had to trust someone, so we chose to trust you, Lord. Do not let us be defeated by our addiction/codependency. Lord, we don't really know you, and we're not sure of how to walk in your ways, yet you are our only hope. When we look at our lives, we only deserve your anger and punishment. We have sinned, and we have been in rebellion and have sought out wrong ways to stop our pain.

We need your forgiveness even though we do not deserve it. Only you, God, can release our feet from the snare of addiction.

One of the greatest fears of codependent/emotionally dependent relationships is that of being left alone—the fear of abandonment.

Oh, Lord, free us from the anguish we feel, the deep emotional upheaval we experience; you are our hope.

Together we can!

Father, it is a joy to know that we are a team working together on my recovery.

Psalm
26

*My feet stand on level ground; in the great
assembly I will praise the Lord. (v. 12)*

My feet stand on level ground. Making a fearless,
searching moral inventory of ourselves, as in Step
Four, will certainly bring us to an awareness of
our humanity. Any pride or ego trip we may have
been on while living in addiction/codependency
comes to a screeching halt. As we look at where
we have been, there is absolutely no room to look
down at others or to judge anyone else. At the
foot of the cross, we all stand on level ground. As
painful as the searching, fearless moral inventory
is, it is not as painful as remaining the same. Once
more we are called upon to face ourselves—to
face what we have done. Then we can admit these
faults and allow God to remove them. Our addic-
tion/codependent nature (behavior) wants to
blame someone else for all of the ills of this life,
but healing will not begin until we are willing to
take responsibility for our behavior and make
amends where we can. Then God can remove
these from us. Pulling these "weeds" from our
lives leaves room for the good fruit to grow.

*God, may I not be content to stay the same but
constantly grow.*

Psalm
27

The Lord is my light and my salvation—
whom shall I fear? The Lord is the
stronghold of my life—of whom shall I be
afraid?
When evil men advance against me to devour
my flesh, when my enemies and my foes
attack me, they will stumble and fall. . . .
Do not hide your face from me, do not turn
your servant away in anger; you have been
my helper. Do not reject me or forsake me,
O God, my Savior.
Though my father and mother forsake me, the
Lord will receive me. (vv. 1–2; 9–10)

The Lord is our stronghold, and unlike the stronghold of addiction, the Lord dispels our unreasonable fears. For many years we have feared everything and everyone, but whom do we fear now? Ourselves.

From time to time, even in recovery, our addictive natures beg and coax and at last attack. But we still do not have to fear. Even when our addiction wants us to turn back, we can still be confident that God is not afraid of the day of trouble. He will keep us safe in his dwelling, in the shelter of his tabernacle. We will triumph over our enemy —this addictive personality.

In our distress we forget that he is near. On some days it seems that we can't find him. Addictive relationships are based on the fear of abandonment and rejection. We cannot have those needs met totally today, but God can ease the fear.

Recovery is important enough to wait for and walk through.

Lord, be a light when my dark emotions cloud my way.

Psalm
28

Hear my cry for mercy as I call to you for help, as I lift up my hands toward your Most Holy Place. (v. 2)

Our emotions speak. Many times in our pain and frustration we call out to the Lord and really expect him not to hear us. We feel unworthy because of our past failures, broken promises, and defeated lives. We are disgusted with ourselves, and we feel sure that he must be, too.

We can each easily say, "I am turning my life, as is, over to God." But this is quite another thing to accomplish. It means coming to someone who knows us completely and trusting that he does want us. It means risking the ultimate rejection— what a task, what a muscle-builder for faith! We are reminded that thousands before us have felt the same way, and when they risked all, they found the Man of Sorrows waiting with arms opened wide. He will not turn us away, and we do not even have to beg him to accept us.

Father, help me to run into your accepting arms.

Psalm
29

The Lord gives strength to his people; the Lord blesses his people with peace. (v. 11)

Only God can change our turmoil into peace, and only he can bring strength into our weakness. But even God cannot do these things for us unless we have put aside our denial facing the reality of our inability to fix our lives or the lives of those we have been codependent upon.

Peace comes when we submit our lives and wills over to the care of God. Peace is the result of surrender, just as turmoil is the result of struggle. Struggle is the result of exerting our wills.

We can *seem* strong; we can *look* strong; but only God can strengthen our weakness. So we bring all that we are and all that we are not to him and allow him to add to us what we lack and remove what we do not need. Yes, God may remove something we are sure we need to live happy and fulfilled lives. But trust him by an act of our wills to do exactly what is good and necessary to promote wholeness.

O God, help me face the truth that I can't do this alone.

Psalm
30

When I felt secure, I said, "I will never be shaken." (v. 6)

Only when our lives are safely in the hands of God can we ever experience true security. In that embrace, we will never be shaken. Notice, it doesn't say we will never *feel shaky,* or *feel shaken.* What we feel in our emotion is not fact but is merely a report of what is happening on the inside of us. Emotions can be the result of something as simple as not eating correctly or on time. Emotions can change with the words or body language of someone we need to affirm us. But because emotions are fickle and subject to change without prior notice, we must remind ourselves that we are held in God's strong embrace, even when our souls tumble uncontrollably.

When we feel that God is not near, we are dismayed. But our feelings can be corrected by what we are saying to ourselves. So we can meditate on the promises of God rather than on "what ifs" or "should haves."

Lord, remind me today that emotions change quickly but you are steadfast.

Psalm
31

*In you, O Lord, I have taken refuge; let me
never be put to shame; deliver me in your
righteousness. (v. 1)*

Shame is one of the most malignant and control-
ling emotions we can experience. Shame brings
us to the misconception that what and who we
are is wrong. In recovery, shame is deadly. Shame
is the stealer of our personhood.

Many times this deep sense of shame is what
first made us reach out to our drug of choice to
ease the inner feeling. When what we are is bad,
there is little hope. If only what we *do* is bad or
wrong, we can hope to change our behavior. But
shame says that *we* are wrong or bad.

Only God can restore our sense of dignity, and
this begins when we can see that he truly wants
to help us. The more aware we become of his desire to be close to us, the less shame we feel.
Shame is healed as we continue to come to him,
as we are, and find him to be completely accepting and totally uncondemning.

*O God, remove my feelings of shame and help
me to forgive myself.*

Psalm
32

*I will instruct you and teach you in the way
   you should go; I will counsel you and watch
   over you.*
*Do not be like the horse or the mule, which have
   no understanding but must be controlled by
   bit and bridle or they will not come to you.*
*Many are the woes of the wicked, but the Lord's
   unfailing love surrounds the man who trusts
   in him. (vv. 8–10)*

God speaks to our hearts just exactly what
we need to hear. On some days in recovery, we
seem to have lost our direction. Our emotions get
topsy-turvy, and we become disoriented. Yet God
says, "On these days I will instruct you and teach
you the way to go." Our Father will talk us
through step by step until once more our lives are
stable and we feel confident. When we don't know
which way to go—when the night is so dark we
can't see—he will not desert us. God knows the
way through the sometimes winding maze of
recovery.

On days when things are better, we have a
tendency to run ahead of God, and in his great
love he holds onto us, even when it seems he is
cramping our style. Just as parents are sometimes
forced to restrain their children, many times it is
in our best interest for God to restrain us.

But always the Lord's unfailing and unconditional love surrounds us, be it in our time of personal inventory, confession, or lack of direction. He surrounds us with his care.

Father, help me to refocus my recovery today.

Psalm
33

For the word of the Lord is right and true; he is
* faithful in all he does.*
The Lord loves righteousness and justice; the
* earth is full of his unfailing love. . . .*
For he spoke, and it came to be; he commanded,
* and it stood firm. (vv. 4–5; 9)*

In the early stages of recovery, we may feel overwhelmed by the pain of our newly awakened feelings. Our drug of choice has kept us conveniently
numbed. It has been so long since we have experienced emotions at all. On days when our pain
seems too big, we may have to consciously turn
our thoughts to his promises. Meditating on those
promises does not instantly bring our lives into
perfection, but stinking thinking must stop somewhere. To redirect our thoughts, to focus our
thoughts on something stable, does eventually
bring order to our disordered lives. At first, we
can only concentrate for short periods of time; but
if we are faithful to this discipline, eventually we
will find that our thinking is easier to turn in the
right direction. Our thoughts do create many of
our emotions.

Lord, today help me to remember your promises
of victory.

Psalm
34

The Lord is close to the brokenhearted and saves
those who are crushed in spirit. . . .
The Lord redeems his servants; no one will be
condemned who takes refuge in him.
(vv. 18; 22)

Not one hurting heart goes unnoticed by him. He is touched by the feelings of our infirmities, and what could be more descriptive of infirmity than the addictive/codependent person? How his heart reaches out to his struggling children over and over. Even in the midst of our addiction/codependency, he longs for us to be whole.

Many times we feel that he hates those of us who are addicts/codependents—but he doesn't. He hates that which is stealing the gift of life from us.

He rescues those who have been crushed in spirit. Is anyone more crushed in spirit than those who have been involved in addiction/codependency? Our own wrong choices have often served as the crushing blow. Yet our Father reaches out to save us even then, even from ourselves.

No one—absolutely no one—will be condemned when we take refuge in him. No matter where we have been, no matter what we have done, no matter how far we have fallen—what a promise! His love reaches out to us, even into the pit of despair to which our addiction/codependency has taken us. His love reaches past all the protective walls we have built and reminds us, "I will not condemn you." Our Father will not condemn us, but what about our own attitude and condemnation? It is so easy for us to hate and to punish ourselves, but that attitude is often projected onto our Father. We condemn ourselves; others may condemn us; but in his hands there is not one tiny bit of condemnation. This freedom from condemnation gives us strength to make amends; the security of acceptance makes it possible to face ourselves and our harmful behavior.

Lord, help me accept myself as human and forgive myself for my humaness.

Psalm
35

*Contend, O Lord, with those who contend with
me; fight against those who fight against
me. (v. 1)*

One of the big things in addiction/codependency
is the tendency to blame our pain on someone
else, anyone else. It is most uncomfortable to take
responsibility for our own mess. Therefore, we
want to fight with those around us; we are angry
and often want revenge on those we feel have
caused our plight. What we are dealing with in
recovery is not a person, place, or thing. We are
dealing with addiction/codependency. Addiction/
codependency is our mortal enemy. Addiction/
codependency is the disease; it is the destroyer.
To fight others is unprofitable. We must face ourselves, our disease—and begin to take responsibility for where we are. Then we must give control
to God, who can save us from ourselves *and* our
disease.

*Lord, it is easier to blame others, but I won't
recover unless I take responsibility for my
behavior. Please help me.*

Psalm
36

How priceless is your unfailing love! Both high
and low among men find refuge in the
shadow of your wings. (v. 7)

There is no partiality with God—whoever comes,
he takes in; whoever is needy, he accepts. We who
knew only death and emptiness find life, and he
gives us light to see.

God holds onto us even when the cravings of
our heart want to yield to the addiction/codepen-
dency. God accepts the high and mighty, and God
accepts the person of low estate. Whoever we are,
he does give us refuge.

Lord, help me to put as high a value on my life
as you do.

Psalm
37

*If the Lord delights in a man's way, he makes
his steps firm. (v. 23)*

Giving God control is a difficult and fearful thing
for those who have spent so much time and effort
trying to be in control. But it is the big step in
recovery that begins the process and the daily
step that keeps us on the journey.

Yes, we may indeed stumble and fall; we may
make mistakes; we may lose our way. But the
good news is that, even if we do, God still holds
onto us. He can set us back on the right path; he
can balance us; he can stabilize us. God will make
these tottering, stumbling steps of recovery into a
firm and solid life-style walk. We do not have to
be defeated.

*Father, thank you for holding onto us on days
we want to run away.*

Psalm
38

*My wounds fester and are loathsome because of
    my sinful folly.
I am bowed down and brought very low; all day
    long I go about mourning.
My back is filled with searing pain; there is no
    health in my body.
I am feeble and utterly crushed; I groan in
    anguish of heart. (vv. 5–8)*

Our bodies, souls, and spirits have been deeply
wounded by our addiction/codependency. The
wounds are infected and loathsome. Many inap-
propriate behaviors are the result of these fester-
ing wounds. Yes, this is the result of our own
willful actions, our sinful follies. This truth must
be faced if recovery progresses. Along with the
fact of our failures and the resulting consequences, we must face still another fact—that we
have to forgive ourselves and stop beating ourselves. Until we have forgiven ourselves, we will
be depressed and angry, which will hinder the
journey of recovery.

Addiction/codependency is a terminal illness
unless we begin to recover. At the beginning, we
are feeble and completely crushed. But our Father,
with our cooperation, can restore us to sanity.

*Lord, please pour the healing oil of your Spirit
into all that is wounded in us today.*

Psalm
39

I said, "I will watch my ways, and keep my
tongue from sin; I will put a muzzle on
my mouth as long as the wicked are in my
presence." (v. 1)

Most of us who are recovering have said the fa-
mous "We can handle it." And we honestly
thought we could. After all, what could be so difficult about this recovery business anyway? In our
hands, our lives are always out of control. That is
so hard for most of us to see, hear, admit, or even
think about. Our life was so unstable—and in reality we had such little control—that the thought of
giving control to another is frightening. But that
is the first step to recovery, where it begins and
how it continues. It is a rude awakening when we
realize how finite our lives really are. Our only
hope is God—someone we cannot see and usually
cannot feel. We must, by a choice of our wills,
accept that he really is and that he is the author
of recovery.

O God, help me remember that when I was in
charge I made a mess.

Psalm
40

I waited patiently for the Lord; he turned to
*   me and heard my cry.*
He lifted me out of the slimy pit, out of the
*   mud and mire; he set my feet on a rock and*
*   gave me a firm place to stand. . . .*
I do not hide your righteousness in my heart; I
*   speak of your faithfulness and salvation. I*
*   do not conceal your love and your truth*
*   from the great assembly. (vv. 1–2; 10)*

Addiction/codependency is a "slimy pit." In that pit is no good thing, no health, no joy, no healthy relationship. In that slimy pit is nothing and no one who is stable. *Unmanageable* could be another word for that state. But God lifts us out. That would be enough—but notice that he goes a step further. He stabilizes and secures us. He takes us out of the quicksand life (addiction/codependency) and gives us a firm place to stand. As recovery progresses, we do begin to sing a new song—it's the song of recovery. In Step Twelve, we take the message to others, and as we reach out to others, using our own story, others find the hope we have, and they begin to trust in God for their recovery.

Taking the message to others keeps us active in our recovery. As we tell others about God's faithfulness in our journey of recovery, we hear it over and over. Everytime we hear it, we are reminded of the hopeless state addiction/codependency had us in; we see God's goodness; and we encourage ourselves.

Reaching out to others keeps recovery fresh.

Lord God, give me words that touch others and that encourage my own recovery.

Psalm
41

*Blessed is he who has regard for the weak; the
    Lord delivers him in times of trouble.
The Lord will protect him and preserve his life;
    he will bless him in the land and not
    surrender him to the desire of his foes.
The Lord will sustain him on his sickbed and
    restore him from his bed of illness.
I said, "O Lord, have mercy on me; heal me, for
    I have sinned against you."
My enemies say of me in malice, "When will he
    die and his name perish?". . .
All my enemies whisper together against me;
    they imagine the worst for me, saying,
"A vile disease has beset him; he will never get
    up from the place where he lies." (vv. 1–5;
    7–8)*

The disease of addiction/codependency is vile.

In our weakness only God is able to deliver us
from the disease. God has protected us and has
preserved our lives many times. We and the disease together have done everything possible to
destroy ourselves. God wants us whole, healed,
delivered, and restored. This is one of those times
when sin requires healing along with forgiveness.

Our enemies are against us, against our recovery. God gives us hope when friends who do not understand discourage us and when the addiction/codependency tries to gain control. God will not let our enemies triumph over us.

Father, thank you for the promise of health and deliverance.

Psalm
42

As the deer pants for streams of water, so my
soul pants for you, O God.
My soul thirsts for God, for the living God.
When can I go and meet with God?
(vv. 1–2)

Seldom do we realize that our innermost being
longs to be filled, but the longing is for far more
than what we find to fill it. It involves so much—
our emptiness from childhood, the pain of our
addiction/codependency, the frustration of recovery. Each thing is felt emotionally and very
strongly. Our being is longing for God. Our soul
is thirsty for him. Yet it seems almost impossible
that we would be able to approach him—at least
our emotions tell us that, because we have strayed
from following him. The memories of what we
have lost haunt us; we suffer depression over our
past. The only hope we have is to put our trust in
God. He is on our side even when we are not. We
often lash out at God, accusing him of forgetting
us. We are convinced he has abandoned us. Today—in spite of what our addiction/codependency
tells us, in spite of what our emotions say—we
can choose to hope in God.

O God, fill all of my empty longings with your
Spirit until I long no more.

Psalm
43

*You are God my stronghold. Why have you
rejected me? Why must I go about
mourning, oppressed by the enemy? (v. 2)*

Many times, especially on those difficult days, it
does feel as though God has rejected us. It seems
we are left alone to battle through. Fear not; feelings never tell us the facts but rather report what
is going on inside of us. God promised not to
leave us, though our feelings say he has. But our
wills decide. We can *choose* to believe his Word, in
spite of what we feel. He has told us the truth.

Mourning and grieving are important aspects
of recovery. Grief is often a normal and healthy
stage of recovery. On the other hand, the "pity
pot" is that destructive "why me?" attitude that
slows down our recovery.

We should allow ourselves to grieve but not to
be consumed by grief. We may let it be a part of
the journey but not the destination.

*Father, help me to know the difference between
grieving and when I am on the "pity pot."*

Psalm
44

It was not by their sword that they won the
*   land, nor did their arm bring them victory;*
*   it was your right hand, your arm, and the*
*   light of your face, for you loved them. . . .*
Awake, O Lord! Why do you sleep? Rouse
*   yourself! Do not reject us forever.*
*   (vv. 3; 23)*

Self-work will not free us from our addiction. But
is not that what the first Step is really saying?
Nothing we can do, nothing we have done has
brought our freedom.

Turning over a million new leaves—a million
broken promises—a million shattered plans: not
once did any of that help. Only when we are convinced that we have *no power* or ability over our
addiction/codependency and when we turn our
lives over to God is there hope for victory. He
gives us this victory because he loves us.

Yet at times we've accused God of taking a nap,
especially when our recovery is not going as we
had planned. Oops! There's the catch; we keep
forgetting who is in charge.

Father, I give you the life I have been unable to
manage. I resign!

Psalm
45

*In your majesty ride forth victoriously in
behalf of truth, humility and righteousness;
let your right hand display awesome
deeds. (v. 4)*

Victory comes in our recovery as the result of
truth, humility, and righteousness.

Truth means we are out of denial: we admitted
we were powerless. We made a decision to turn
our lives and wills over to the care of God. We
made a fearless, searching moral inventory. Then
we made a list of all the people we had wronged
and became willing to make direct amends. Now
we continue to take a personal inventory and,
when wrong, promptly admit it.

These steps help us become humble. Who can
look honestly at the messes we've made and remain proud? Righteousness cannot be attained by
our own works but is a gift that is ours as a result
of Steps Two through Eleven. It is the fruit of
recovery.

*Lord, some days I want to hide from life. Give
me courage to face reality.*

Psalm
46

God is our refuge and strength, an ever-present
help in trouble.
Therefore we will not fear, though the earth give
way and the mountains fall into the heart of
the sea,
though its waters roar and foam and the
mountains quake with their surging. . . .
Be still, and know that I am God; I will be
exalted among the nations, I will be exalted
in the earth. (vv. 1–3; 10)

It can become a great comfort to our trembling,
fearful heart to know that God wants to be a refuge and strength, a constant help when we are in
trouble—especially when the trouble is the result
of our foolish living and wrong choices.

Even when we find ourselves in the midst of a
personal earthquake, we can rest in his promise
to keep us safe. We can know that there is a river
of safety, a place of security, hidden away in the
safety of God. God is our fortress, our safe place,
our comfortable place. When we've stood all the
pain we can, when we feel like a lost, frightened
child, when we are confused and hurt—we can
run to the safety of God's arms.

Stop! Be still! Look! Look at the lives of those who are successful in their journeys of recovery. Look, see how much peace replaced that inner turmoil. *Be still and know*—be still and meditate on him.

O God, develop in me the ability to trust in your power to see me through the earthquakes in my life.

Psalm
47

*Clap your hands, all you nations; shout to God
with cries of joy. (v. 1)*

On the days when we feel well and the family isn't
in turmoil, it is easy to clap our hands and shout
to God with cries of joy. And just as there are bad
days, there are good days in recovery. Perhaps today is not a good one—and to praise God seems
ludicrous. Many times recovery requires us to
stretch beyond the comfortable, to step when we'd
rather sit, to praise when we'd rather whine or
grumble. But to praise in the midst of our trouble,
pain, or discouragement is a sacrifice of praise. To
speak positive words even when we don't feel
them, begins a change in our emotion. So even if
this is not a day that would ordinarily evoke
praise, why not by an act of our will begin to
praise God? For what? Look at where we have
been, where we are today, and where we are
heading. Now look at where we were and the direction we'd be going if God had not reached into
the pit to rescue us. Is that not worth a few shouts
of praise?

*O God, give me a voice to praise you in the
midst of my brokenness.*

Psalm
48

Within your temple, O God, we meditate on
your unfailing love. . . .
For this God is our God for ever and ever; he
will be our guide even to the end.
(vv. 9; 14)

To meditate requires discipline that few of us pos-
sess at the beginning of our recovery. Maybe that
is why this is Step Eleven and not Step Three. To
meditate means to stop, to sit long enough in
God's presence to quiet the rushing thoughts, and
to center (lock in) on a God who loves us uncon-
ditionally. To do this brings a stability into our
lives that we have not had before. To renew our
minds from the old thinking—that God is absent,
angry, or hates us—into correct thinking about
his *unfailing love* brings a peace that we need in
order to continue our recovery.

To meditate means to keep mulling over and
over, to remind ourselves continually of God's
love and care.

God is the only one who can and who is willing
to guide us out of the mess we've found ourselves
in through our addiction/codependency.

Lord, I've never learned to be still and know
you. Teach me now, please.

Psalm
49

My mouth will speak words of wisdom; the
utterance from my heart will give
understanding. . . .
Why should I fear when evil days come, when
wicked deceivers surround me. . . .
No man can redeem the life of another or give
God a ransom for him. . . .
But God will redeem my life from the grave; he
will surely take me to himself. (vv. 3; 5;
7; 15)

Listen to the unrehearsed words that come "un-bidden" from the inner being. If we watch reactions that come spontaneously, we will have an understanding of the way things really are deep inside. Our reactions expose the real us. Part of Step Ten is to continue to take a personal inventory. To evaluate our unplanned reactions will help us do this.

Bad days will come during our recovery. Some days we will want to give up. Some days it will seem we have lost all the ground we had gained. But don't be fooled, don't stop, don't quit! Get back up, regather your resources, and move on. Temporary setbacks are just that.

Caretakers have the mistaken idea that they can love or give or do enough to make the addict well. Many become codependent because of this false belief.

God will redeem our lives from destruction. He will deliver us. He will teach us how to live.

Lord, give me strength to get up one more time than I fall.

Psalm
50

*"Gather to me my consecrated ones, who made
 a covenant with me by sacrifice."*
*And the heavens proclaim his righteousness, for
 God himself is judge. (vv. 5–6)*

Every word of this psalm seems to scorch, yet
they are true of our addictive/codependent nature.

That part of our being is selfish, self-gratifying,
and will stop at nothing to satisfy the craving—
we would lie, manipulate, cheat, control, or bar-
gain. These are practices in our old nature that do
not cease just because we decide to recover but
must be brought to death daily through a moral
inventory. Facing ourselves is difficult to do but is
certainly a big and important daily step.

*Father, aid me as I search out the inner depths
of my heart.*

Psalm
51

*Have mercy on me, O God, according to your
unfailing love; according to your great
compassion blot out my transgressions.*

*Wash away all my iniquity and cleanse me from
my sin.*

*For I know my transgressions, and my sin is
always before me. . . .*

*Surely you desire truth in the inner parts; you
teach me wisdom in the inmost place.*

*Cleanse me with hyssop, and I will be clean;
wash me, and I will be whiter than
snow. . . .*

*Hide your face from my sins and blot out all
my iniquity. . . .*

*Restore to me the joy of your salvation and
grant me a willing spirit, to sustain me.*

*Then I will teach transgressors your ways, and
sinners will turn back to you. . . .*

*The sacrifices of God are a broken spirit; a
broken and contrite heart, O God, you will
not despise. (vv. 1–3; 6–7; 9; 12–13; 17)*

One way of admitting that we are powerless
would be to ask God to have mercy on us. "Wash
away all my iniquity and cleanse me from my sin"
is certainly a verbal declaration of our faith that
God can restore us. Asking him to forgive and

help us begins the process of turning our lives and wills over to God. David certainly made a fearless, searching, moral inventory of his life as he realized his transgressions and was quick to admit to God and to himself what a mess he was in. We have to get there, too. We are ready to have God remove these defects when we say along with David, "hide your face from my sins and blot out all my iniquity." After our spiritual awakening, we do want to tell fellow strugglers that it is possible to be free. What a beautiful summation of the Twelve Steps David gives us in this psalm.

God, I need your help in working these Steps rather than taking a shortcut.

Psalm
52

Why do you boast of evil, you mighty man?
Why do you boast all day long, you who are
a disgrace in the eyes of God? . . .
"Here now is the man who did not make God
his stronghold but trusted in his great
wealth and grew strong by destroying
others!"
But I am like an olive tree flourishing in the
house of God; I trust in God's unfailing love
for ever and ever.
I will praise you forever for what you have
done; in your name I will hope, for your
name is good. I will praise you in the
presence of your saints. (vv. 1; 7–9)

Boasting is a symptom of poor self-esteem and low self-worth. Being addicts/codependents, our self-concepts are not usually very good. One unhealthy and nonproductive way of handling poor self-esteem is to brag. But look at the end of boasting: Our tongues cannot save us, change us, or deliver us from a poor self-image. They will only cover up. Speaking the truth about ourselves is so difficult; it hurts too badly to see who we really are. God desires to destroy that false, wrong self-image so that it will stop producing sour fruit in our lives. Boasting ends with us still trusting in something we do that makes us feel a little better

but also may include putting others down and be-
littling. Trusting in self is disastrous.

But when we do trust in what God says about
us, we realize he has spoken our worth as a person by his sacrifice for us.

*God, give me eyes to see myself the way you do
and to voice your truth instead of boasting.*

Psalm
53

There they were, overwhelmed with dread,
where there was nothing to dread. God
scattered the bones of those who attacked
you; you put them to shame, for God
despised them. (v. 5)

Often in our recovery we are overwhelmed with
dread. Our feelings are waking up, and we are
more in touch with the negative emotions. We are
full of dread, full of "what ifs" and full of "should
haves." But we cannot deal with abstracts—we
can only deal with reality. Dread is the emotion
that steals the joy from everyday living and hinders our journey of recovery.

Whatever our reality is today, God gives us
strength and courage to face it and overcome it.
Much of what we fear never happens, and we
spend endless energy trying to deal with imagi-
nary possibilities.

Father, teach me how to lay aside the "what ifs"
and "should haves" and face life realistically.

Psalm
54

*Strangers are attacking me; ruthless men seek
my life—men without regard for God.
Surely God is my help; the Lord is the one who
sustains me. . . .
For he has delivered me from all my troubles,
and my eyes have looked in triumph on my
foes. (vv. 3–4; 7)*

Our battle is not with human beings—our battle
is with our own stinking thinking, our own inability and unwillingness to let go and let God.
We must release our desire to control and manipulate. That frees us to do battle against the *real
enemy*. God is willing to deliver us from all the
troubles we have encountered as a result of our
addiction/codependency. But it is not an instant,
quick fix, a guaranteed no-pain way to happiness.
It happens as we are faithful to our program.
Working those Steps daily, recovery happens
"here a little, there a little," in twenty-four-hour-
a-day, one-day-at-a-time segments.

*Lord, sometimes I'd like to skip over the
mundane Steps of recovery. Help me stick to the
Steps faithfully.*

Psalm
55

Listen to my prayer, O God, do not ignore my
*   plea;*
hear me and answer me. My thoughts
*   trouble me and I am distraught*
at the voice of the enemy, at the stares of the
*   wicked; for they bring down suffering upon*
*   me and revile me in their anger. (vv. 1–3)*

On some days, we feel that God is probably sick of hearing from us. Like parents who tire of answering a child's endless "why's," it feels like he is ignoring us.

Once more we have fallen prey to crazy thinking, and we are relying on our emotions for the truth. Stinking thinking does trouble us, because those thoughts do not go in the same direction as our recovery is going. Indeed, our heart is in anguish; we have not left behind a drink, drug, or relationship but a life-style. At times we may feel we will die, and yet we are afraid we won't die. It's natural to want to run away and hide, but this problem of addiction/codependency can't be run from—it must be conquered. Even in that, we have to go back to our own personal powerlessness and God's ability to restore us to sanity.

Lord, what a humbling experience to realize that
I need your help in conquering this disease.

Psalm
56

*My slanderers pursue me all day long; many
are attacking me in their pride. (v. 2)*

Our slanderers are not powerful outside forces;
the real slanderers come from our own self-talk.
There is the real problem. Self-esteem and self-
worth respond to what we say to ourselves about
ourselves, about our recovery, about life, and
about God. Whatever we tell ourselves affects the
way we view and feel about ourselves. We give
others the power to determine how we view ourselves as people. When these others affirm us, we
feel good about ourselves; when they withhold
positive comments or responses, we feel bad. We
may then work even harder to get the response
we want. The one positive response we need most
is not our spouse's, friends', parents', or employ-
er's—it is our own! So why not begin to say some
good things to yourself about "yours truly?"

*Father, teach me to embrace what you say,
especially when it isn't what I want to hear.*

Psalm
57

Have mercy on me, O God, have mercy on me,
for in you my soul takes refuge. I will take
refuge in the shadow of your wings until the
disaster has passed.
I cry out to God Most High, to God, who
fulfills his purpose for me. (vv. 1–2)

Often our self-esteem is so low because of the big
mess we made during the days before recovery.
Therefore, it is difficult to remember that God's
mercy never ends. We cannot exhaust it! Maybe
we have a tendency to think (feel) about God's
mercy in the same way we extend mercy to others.
But our God is the expert on mercy; he always has
more than enough. Most of us have a tendency to
take refuge in God as long as the storm lasts or
the disaster lasts; but we get into trouble when we
venture out of the safety of totally depending
on him.

Anytime the pain becomes too intense, we can
cry out to God, who has a purpose for us and
who is faithful to fulfill it—if we cooperate. We
may lose sight of his plan or purpose, but he never does. On our most bewildering, confusing days
he knows where we are going and how to get us
there.

O God, help me to accept the mercy that you
constantly extend to me.

Psalm
58

Do you rulers indeed speak justly? Do you
*   judge uprightly among men?*
No, in your heart you devise injustice, and
*   your hands mete out violence on the earth.*
Even from birth the wicked go astray, from the
*   womb they are wayward and speak lies.*
*   (vv. 1–3)*

In our own hearts, we are very hard on ourselves.
We are not fair; we are not just. We strike out at
ourselves with cruel words, hateful remarks, and
behaviors that punish. From some of our earliest
memories comes the feeling that we are worthless. What rules our recovery? Who is king over
the enemy of addiction/codependency when we
think we are in charge? When we do not work our
program? When we forget that we are absolutely
powerless over addiction/codependency? If we follow our own hearts, we will fail.

Our best efforts will not carry us through as
addicts/codependents; it is a most difficult thing
to place trust in someone other than ourselves.
Giving control to someone else is frightening because for so long our lives have been out of control while we thought we were in control. God our
Father is the only one able to bring control, as we
allow him to rule as king in our recovery.

Father, today I resign as king, and I appoint
you to rule my recovery.

Psalm
59

*Deliver me from my enemies, O God; protect
me from those who rise up against me.
(v. 1)*

Many times our addiction/codependency began
because of painful emotions we had tried to cover
up or numb out. Therefore, we now see emotions
as the enemy; we run from pain. Guilt, shame,
failure, and confusion all work together to keep
us from recovering. That little wounded child inside of us is so ashamed because he or she seems
to be so bad. For many of us, there was no emotionally whole parent who could help dispel our
fears about life and help us see that we were not
responsible for someone else's pain.

In recovery, we must make peace with that little
wounded child of our past, allowing God to be
that parent who loves and nurtures. We must face
the hurtful events and emotions of the past—and
once and for all deal with and cut free from yesterday to face the possibility of recovery today.

*O God, please cut me free from yesterday
through resolving those hurtful issues.*

Psalm
60

*You have rejected us, O God, and burst
forth upon us; you have been angry—now
restore us!*
*You have shaken the land and torn it open;
mend its fractures, for it is quaking. . . .*
*Give us aid against the enemy, for the help of
man is worthless.*
*With God we will gain the victory, and he will
trample down our enemies. (vv. 1–2; 11–12)*

The still "unrecovering" part of us speaks the fear,
doubt, and unbelief that we hold in our hearts.
That unhealthy part fears that God has rejected
us and has abused us and is angry. But we continue to cry out for restoration with that part of us
that is healthy.

Our unhealthy part continues its stinking thinking—feeling that it is God who has shaken us,
torn our lives open. The recovering part of us
knows that it is only God who can set us free,
that even in the midst of our addiction he does
love us.

Oftentimes we accuse God of leaving us, but
actually we are the ones who distanced ourselves
from God, possibly because of our shame and
feelings of guilt over our past.

Yet recovery continues when we realize once more that he is the only one who can truly set us free. Only God can trample down the enemy of addiction/codependence.

Father, please remind me that you are near, regardless of what my emotions tell me.

Psalm
61

Hear my cry, O God; listen to my prayer.
From the ends of the earth I call to you, I call
*   as my heart grows faint; lead me to the rock*
*   that is higher than I.*
For you have been my refuge, a strong tower
*   against the foe.*
I long to dwell in your tent forever and take
*   refuge in the shelter of your wings.*
*   (vv. 1–4)*

While our spirits long for communion with God, our flesh struggles against it. Our flesh, as always, wants to be in control, wants to be gratified. Most of us did not call on God until we had grown so faint that we knew we were going to die. We cry out only when we realize that we are truly powerless over our addiction/codependency.

But in our faint condition, it is good to know there is a rock that is stronger than we have ever been. It is that rock that is our refuge, our strong tower, and our shelter. Our rock is always open for us. This becomes more and more evident as we recover and practice coming to him and find he is there.

Father, help me to accept my weakness as a gift
that directs me to your strength.

Psalm
62

*My soul finds rest in God alone; my salvation
comes from him.
He alone is my rock and my salvation; he is my
fortress, I will never be shaken. (vv. 1–2)*

". . . In God alone." What a sobering thought and
yet how true. Our salvation comes from God; deliverance comes from God; recovery comes from
God. Our souls can rest in God alone. He alone
is our rock, salvation, and fortress. Even our
worth as people is determined by God alone, and
as we turn to him, he reminds us that he loves us
as we are.

Only as we daily walk in the Twelve Steps, reminding ourselves that God alone is able to truly
change us, can we know that we will not be shak-
en. Only as we submit to his leadership and obey
his instruction can we be assured of success in our
journey of recovery.

God alone plus one willing person equals recovery today.

*Lord, help me join forces with your plan of
recovery for my life.*

Psalm
63

O God, you are my God, earnestly I seek you;
my soul thirsts for you, my body longs for
you, in a dry and weary land where there is
no water. . . .
I will praise you as long as I live, and in your
name I will lift up my hands. . . .
On my bed I remember you; I think of you
through the watches of the night. . . .
My soul clings to you; your right hand upholds
me. (vv. 1; 4; 6; 8)

What a beautiful description of Steps Two, Three, Eleven, and Twelve. Convinced that we can reach out to God, we begin to earnestly seek him, longing for him, thirsting for him. Our lives were so dry and so empty, and we began to come to an awareness that he was just waiting to fill that which was empty, satisfy that which longs.

Many a night's sleep escapes us as we go over and over things we cannot change, but what a difference those sleepless nights can bring if we begin instead to meditate on God, who is the author and finisher of our recovery. Often as addicts and codependents we want to cling to someone or something—but as we improve our knowing of God, we learn to cling to him. How tightly he holds us to his bosom as we draw from him the strength to face a new day of recovery.

O Lord, give me strength to turn to you, the author and finisher of my recovery.

Psalm
64

Hear me, O God, as I voice my complaint;
protect my life from the threat of the
enemy. . . .
All mankind will fear; they will proclaim the
works of God and ponder what he has
done. (vv. 1; 9)

Addiction/codependency is our mortal enemy, and that enemy stands ready to steal our very lives if we allow it. This disease is progressive—and, yes, it is terminal.

That part of us that does not want to recover conspires against us. It sharpens tongues like swords, and aiming words like arrows, it shoots at us. It plots injustice. It does *anything* to convince us that this recovery is not all it's cracked up to be; it's too hard, too painful.

We must be aware of the truth and continue to work toward recovery. The Twelve Steps keep us in touch with the fact that we must cooperate with God to keep the enemy defeated.

Sharing the message of hope with someone else keeps us on the pathway as we hear our own story over and over; we not only encourage others but ourselves as well.

God, be patient to continually remind me that I
must cooperate with you.

Psalm
65

O you who hear prayer, to you all men will
come.
When we were overwhelmed by sins, you
forgave our transgressions . . . who stilled
the roaring of the seas, the roaring of their
waves, and the turmoil of the nations.
(vv. 2–3; 7)

How wonderful is the hope that, no matter what
kind of mess we are in, God is still merciful and
desires to forgive us and remove the stain of our
sin—the guilt and shame of our failure. The only
thing that stands as a hindrance is our unwillingness or inability to forgive ourselves. Until we are
able to forgive ourselves, we will never enjoy the
peace he wants us to enjoy. Sometimes when we
are working Step Six, we need to also work Steps
Eight and Nine—but toward ourselves. Our Father wants us to enjoy life, but guilt of the past
will steal this gift. What a shame that we hold
ourselves in prison when he has so willingly
opened the prison door. So why not work those
Steps into self-forgiveness and step into freedom?

Lord, teach me the difference between forgiving
myself and excusing myself.

Psalm
66

Come and see what God has done, how awesome
his works in man's behalf! . . .he has
preserved our lives and kept our feet from
slipping. . . .
I will come to your temple with burnt offerings
and fulfill my vows to you. . . .
Praise be to God, who has not rejected my
prayer or withheld his love from me!
(vv. 5; 9; 13; 20)

When we look at where we were *before* recovery
and compare it to where we are *now*, we'll know
for sure that he was the only one who could do
it! In our lives as recovering addicts/codepen-
dents, we know that his deeds are awesome, his
power is great. So often he has preserved our
lives, even when we were ready for a major fall.
He helped us find a better way.

One of our behaviors as addicts/codependents
is to blame others, blame anyone and everyone for
anything and everything. We even try to blame
God. But even so, he brings us to a place of abun-
dance (v. 12).

In the bargaining stage of recovery, we often make promises to God. Some we need to keep, but others we need to lay aside for what they were—words of bargaining that resulted from the pain we were feeling.

God never withholds his love from us, but often the pain is so intense we may not feel his love and care. Still, he is there, loving us back to life.

O God, constantly remind me of the place from which you have brought me.

Psalm
67

*May God be gracious to us and bless us and
make his face shine upon us, that your
ways may be known on earth, your
salvation among all nations. (vv. 1–2)*

A grateful heart is always in order, but for those
who are in pain, or in the earlier stages of recovery, it may be difficult to thank and praise. But
even in our brokenness, praise is good.

Praise brings the presence of God into our sit-
uation; praise is positive force against negative
happenings and the resulting emotions. Praise is
verbally expressing what God has done in our
lives. Praise is one way of getting the message to
others when we are working the Twelve Steps.

Why not replace grumbling with praise and see
if there isn't much more joy and peace inside our
hearts?

*Father, help praise come from my lips, especially
at the times I'd rather complain.*

Psalm
68

A father to the fatherless, a defender of widows,
is God in his holy dwelling.
God sets the lonely in families, he leads forth
the prisoners with singing; but the rebellious
live in a sun-scorched land. (vv. 5–6)

Many of us who are recovering were raised in alcoholic, dysfunctional, or neurotic families. As a result, we may have felt like we were the parent. We had little emotional support, little nurture, because one parent was dysfunctional and the other parent was codependent—taking care of and trying to control the other parent's behavior. So that left us as children to try to figure life out. But in recovery, God will himself parent us and teach us how to be a parent to that little wounded child inside. God places us in spiritual families (local fellowships) to further our growth. Whether it is our church family or support group, they become our family in recovery.

Lord, help me to learn that you are the only
perfect parent.

Psalm
69

*Save me, O God, for the waters have come up
to my neck. I sink in the miry depths,
where there is no foothold.
I have come into the deep waters; the floods
engulf me.
I am worn out calling for help; my throat
is parched. My eyes fail, looking for
my God. . . .
You know my folly, O God; my guilt is not
hidden from you. . . .
I am a stranger to my brothers, an alien to
my own mother's sons. (vv. 1–3; 5; 8)*

We are reminded in Steps Eight and Nine that
sobriety brings with it a new dimension: facing
what we have not faced before, feeling those emotions that have been stuffed down and denied.
When this happens *it does* feel as if the waters are
going to overwhelm us.

Addiction steals from us, but we have to pay
the price for what has been stolen; many times
restitution is only the beginning of the price we
must pay.

God indeed knows our folly; he is aware of our guilt, and yet he still wants us. Only God understands us completely, and only he can free us. Our addiction/codependency destroys our ability to have intimate relationships with anyone. But as we are faithful to work that eighth and ninth Step, God is able to use this most humbling experience to build bridges over the wide gulf between us and those we have hurt.

God, sometimes it seems that my emotions are too much. Help me process them and let them go.

Psalm
70

Hasten, O God, to save me; O Lord, come
  quickly to help me. . . .
Yet I am poor and needy; come quickly to me, O
  God. You are my help and my deliverer; O
  Lord, do not delay. . . . (vv. 1; 5)

Instant healing—we all wish for it. But like many
instant foods, there seems to be something miss-
ing. God works in our lives in times and seasons,
and we don't have to remind him how badly we
hurt or for how long we have suffered. We don't
even have to refresh his memory on how desper-
ately we want to be whole. If there seems to be a
delay, there is a reason. Many of the lessons we
learn in patience will bless us later. When we are
poor and needy, we do want a quick fix. Hurry,
hurry, hurry and make this pain stop. Isn't that
how we got into our addiction/codependency in
the first place? So we need to

- slow down,
- stop chomping at the bit,
- wait,
- remember.

God is the one in charge of our recovery, and he
knows exactly how to direct us so that we recover
on a daily basis.

Lord, teach me to rest when there is a delay.

Psalm 71

In you, O Lord, I have taken refuge; let me
never be put to shame. . . .
For you have been my hope, O Sovereign
Lord, my confidence since my youth.
From birth I have relied on you; you brought
me forth from my mother's womb. I will
ever praise you. . . .
Do not cast me away when I am old; do not
forsake me when my strength is gone.
(vv. 1; 5–6; 9)

When we make a decision to turn our lives and
wills over to God, we are able to take refuge in
the Lord. Only then can there be any continuing
wholeness. We have learned in Step-One living
that whatever is done in our own strength is as
fickle as the wind. Our strength fails all too
quickly.

Hope—what a wonderful word and what an attitude to have toward God. He is our hope of recovery. He is our confidence for the future.

When we have strength, we are going to fall
back into "I can handle it," so it is a blessing if we
have no strength. We can be assured that he will
not forsake us even at our weakest moments. The
most important emotion in recovery is hope.

Lord, I ask you to restore my ability to hope,
especially when I feel hopeless.

Psalm
72

*He will defend the afflicted among the people
and save the children of the needy. . . .
For he will deliver the needy who cry out, the
afflicted who have no one to help.
He will take pity on the weak and the needy
and save the needy from death.
He will rescue them from oppression and
violence, for precious is their blood in his
sight. (vv. 4; 12–14)*

The words *afflicted, needy,* and *weak,* which appear
in these verses—what a description of our powerlessness and unmanageable lives before recovery. *Defend, save, deliver,* and *rescue* are words that
describe the results of turning our lives and wills
over to God in recovery.

God is on our side; he is not against us. What a
comfort to begin to learn this. As addicted/code-
pendent people, we have hated ourselves so much
that it is a comfort to realize he does not hate us.
God wants to deliver us, the afflicted, needy, and
weak. He will strengthen that which is weak; he
will fulfill that which is needy and deliver us from
the affliction of addiction/codependency.

*Lord, you are on my side. Help me to be on my
side, too.*

Psalm
73

*For I envied the arrogant when I saw the
  prosperity of the wicked.*
*They have no struggles; their bodies are healthy
  and strong. . . .*
*This is what the wicked are like—always
  carefree, they increase in wealth.*
*Surely in vain have I kept my heart pure; in
  vain have I washed my hands in
  innocence.* (vv. 3–4; 12–13)

Continuing a *personal* inventory will keep us busy.
Getting our eyes on others is always a poor
choice. Trying to work someone else's program
will cause us to get bogged down. It is easy to get
resentful toward those who *seem* to be free and
those who have not suffered as we have.

It seems. . . . It feels. . . . We assume. . . .

These three statements get recovering people into
trouble every time. Look at verse 12: The wicked
seem to be "always carefree [and increasing] in
wealth." It *feels* that we have kept our hearts pure
in vain. We *assume* that this is the way it is.

Sometimes in our pain we are angry with God,
and yet he holds onto us, guides us. Our strength
will fail, but God's strength will not fail. It is good
to be near God.

*O God, help me to be honest about my
inventory and faithful to work my program.*

Psalm
74

Your foes roared in the place where you met
* with us; they set up their standards as signs.*
They behaved like men wielding axes to cut
* through a thicket of trees.*
They smashed all the carved paneling with their
* axes and hatchets.*
They burned your sanctuary to the ground;
* they defiled the dwelling place of your Name.*
They said in their hearts, "We will crush them
* completely!" They burned every place where*
* God was worshiped in the land. (vv. 4–8)*

Not only is our addiction/codependency our enemy, but it is also God's enemy because it steals us from him. We are bound with iron fetters to something as insignificant as a drink . . . a drug . . . a circumstance . . . a relationship . . . an activity—something that will consume and control us.

Addiction/codependency mocks us! How simple it would be for God to take his hand and wipe out the disease, yet he doesn't do it that way. It is a tiny step here, another step there, a larger step somewhere else. It is a new attitude: learning to rest instead of struggle. Coming to know that only God can set us free as we cooperate with him on a daily basis is growth in him.

Lord, help me to be grateful for the daily,
seemingly insignificant steps of recovery.

Psalm
75

You say, "I choose the appointed time; it is I who judge uprightly." (v. 2)

"The appointed time"—yet much of our frustration in recovery comes from our trying to push and pull, trying to force recovery at a faster pace. We all want too much too soon, but that buildup can cause us to relapse. Babies grow and develop at their own pace, and all the bragging mamas in the world can't circumvent that baby's speed. Sometimes children miss a step or stage of development, and they have other problems later on. So it is with our recovery. One Step builds upon another; one Step compliments the former Step. Step One without Step Two is worthless. Steps are just that—steps. Each addict/codependent is an individual (unique)—a one-of-a-kind designer's original. Each person recovers at his or her own speed. Our "appointed time" includes where we are today—not one Step is wasted; each is important. God's timetable is usually quite different from ours, but his is always "right on schedule."

God, help me not to balk but to walk,
step by step.

Psalm
76

When you, O God, rose up to judge, to save all
the afflicted of the land. . . .
He breaks the spirit of rulers; he is feared by the
kings of the earth (vv. 9; 12)

Surely no afflictions affect more people than addiction and codependency. Millions of people are affected in some way. Either they are addicts, they live with an addict, or they were raised by an addict. Addiction has indeed ruled our lives and controlled our emotions, and we have struggled to get free or to get others free. Only God is able to break the spirit of the addiction that has been the ruler of our lives.

If we try to rule, we are controlled; if we allow God to rule, we are free. So it's an easy choice to make, or at least it should be.

God, give me grace to resign and allow
you to rule.

Psalm
77

I cried out to God for help; I cried out to God to
hear me.
When I was in distress, I sought the Lord; at
night I stretched out untiring hands and my
soul refused to be comforted. (vv. 1–2)

Sad to say, but for most of us, only distress in our
addicted/codependent circumstances will bring us
to the place of recovery. Some days during our
recovery are intense with pain.

- spiritual
- relational
- emotional
- physical
- financial

The pain may cause tears, praying, and crying
out for help. When we experience the pain, it may
register as God's anger or his punishment, but not
so. It is God's mercy, even "severe mercy," which
brings us to the end of ourselves. The pain and
difficulty then become, not a negative, but a positive thing, because it brought us a life-changing,
full-of-hope pathway into recovery.

Don't waste pain; look for a doorway into new
areas of recovery.

Lord, I thank you for the distress that brought
me to recovery.

Psalm
78

. . . what we have heard and known, what our
fathers have told us.
We will not hide them from their children; we
will tell the next generation the
praiseworthy deeds of the Lord, his power,
and the wonders he has done. (vv. 3–4)

This entire psalm is the history of God's faithfulness to his rebellious, hard-headed, stubborn children. Reading it, we find the miracles performed over and over, his anger, his correction. But most of all, we see his faithfulness—*in spite of how the "kids" acted*. These stories were to be passed on from generation to generation and family to family. Likewise, our stories of recovery should be passed on to others who are still struggling and have not chosen the way of recovery, as well as to others well into recovery. Names, dates, and places are different, but the up-and-down struggle is very similar. We are encouraged when we hear of someone else who felt what we are feeling and has experienced victory.

Sharing our Step Twelve with others, sharing the "good news" of recovery with others—that God loves addicts/codependents and has a plan to get us free—gives hope to those who are still struggling. We need to share our stories with our children because we know that addiction is a disease passed on to the next generation. The principles of recovery can also be passed along in just the same way.

Father, let my story of recovery make others aware of your faithfulness.

Psalm
79

Help us, O God our Savior, for the glory of
your name; deliver us and forgive our sins
for your name's sake. . . .
Then we your people, the sheep of your
pasture, will praise you forever; from
generation to generation we will recount
your praise. (vv. 9; 13)

To admit to God, ourselves, and to another human that we are wrong is a real pride killer. As difficult as it is to come to that place, it is even more difficult to allow God to remove these defects. Yet our desperate need makes us ready.

To know that we need surgery is sobering. But to actually be wheeled down the hall, have the IV inserted, and wait for the anesthesia to put us under is a new ball game altogether. Waking up to the postsurgical pain, however, is hardest of all.

Allowing God to remove these defects of character would be no problem at all if he could just instantly wave his hand. But he is removing diseased habit-structures, and this soul surgery is painful. The promise is that, when we have recovered, we will have the ability to live life without being bogged down with the excess luggage. We will praise God and be joyful; we can share the story of recovery with others who travel along this same pathway.

Father, give me strength of spirit to endure the healing pain.

Psalm
80

Restore us, O God; make your face shine upon
us, that we may be saved. . . .
Then we will not turn away from you; revive
us, and we will call on your name.
(vv. 3; 18)

The theme of recovery is restoration. Addiction/
codependency is the destroyer, the stealer, the author of ruined lives, families, and people. What a
blessing to realize that God can and will restore
and revive.

"Restore us, O God" is the prayer of recovery;
not "fix" us, not merely stop the pain, but rather
restore and remake us. Remodel our thinking, our
mind-set, renew our spirit, and rekindle our zest
for living. That prayer is one that our Father delights in answering.

The problem is never with God but is with our unreal expectations of how this restoration should take place and within the time frame we have allotted. Restoration is not a quick, prefabricated project that is thrown together. It is a deliberate and planned removal of the unwanted, a detailed refining of that which is to be preserved, and an addition of that which was not before. Restoration in recovery is similar—removing defects of character, correcting stinking thinking, and giving us hope we've never experienced.

Lord, teach me to wait for restoration when my impatience is crying for a quick fix.

Psalm
81

But my people would not listen to me; Israel
would not submit to me.
So I gave them over to their stubborn hearts to
follow their own devices.
If my people would but listen to me, if Israel
would follow my ways, how quickly would I
subdue their enemies and turn my hand
against their foes! (vv. 11–14)

It is a major accomplishment to turn our will over
to God. We are stubborn people, and we want
things our way, even recovery. One of our down-
falls in recovery is that we resist listening to God.
The voice of our enemy—our voice, the voice of
defeat—we will hear, but we have trouble listening to God. Could that be because his voice
speaks hope, and we feel hopeless? His voice
speaks reality, and we live in denial? His voice corrects, and we don't want to change? His voice also
tells us who we really are, and his voice reminds
us that he sees us differently than others view us.

Recovery would progress much quicker if only
we would listen to God. When we listen to God,
we learn to follow his ways, and that brings our
enemy of addiction/codependency to an abrupt
end. *Let's stop and listen to our Father today* and allow his Words to encourage and strengthen us.

O God, atune my ears to hear your voice.

Psalm
82

Defend the cause of the weak and fatherless;
*   maintain the rights of the poor and*
*   oppressed.*
Rescue the weak and needy; deliver them from
*   the hand of the wicked.*
They know nothing, they understand nothing.
*   They walk about in darkness; all the*
*   foundations of the earth are shaken. (vv. 3–5)*

Many addicts/codependents were raised in dysfunctional or alcoholic homes. Adult children of alcoholic/dysfunctional families are still little children inside. Weak and fatherless, we became poor, oppressed, and very needy. Most of us seek some way outside of God to fill this need, and thus we have delivered ourselves into the control of addiction/codependency ("the wicked"). Our Father will deliver us from the hand of the wicked if we will only come to him.

It is a very humbling experience to realize that we are in control of only one thing—admitting that we are powerless. Yet in that admission we place ourselves in a position to be a child with our

Father, having these previously unmet needs met. As the little wounded child within is nurtured and becomes whole, the adult begins to walk consistently in recovery. God delights in our being a child with him.

Father, help me to place myself in the position of being your child today.

Psalm
83

O God, do not keep silent; be not quiet, O God,
be not still. (v. 1)

Many times we want to help our Father "hurry
up." We want to be on God's vengeance team, and
most certainly we want to tell him how to do
things. Is that still our addictive/codependent nature trying to be in control—even of God? For so
long in our codependency we have tried to run
the show by telling others what they *should* do or
what they need to do. From time to time we forget
that we can't even run our own lives. How ludicrous that we have made such a mess of everything in our lives and would think we could help
even one person straighten out his or her situa-
tion. But, oh, how we try.

God knows how to run his universe; he knows
who needs what and exactly when certain things
need to happen.

So what can we do? Turn our lives and wills
over to God and resign our positions as assistants
to God.

Lord, are you absolutely sure you can handle
my recovery?

Psalm
84

My soul yearns, even faints, for the courts of
the Lord; my heart and my flesh cry out for
the living God. . . .
As they pass through the Valley of Baca, they
make it a place of springs; the autumn
rains also cover it with pools.
They go from strength to strength, till each
appears before God in Zion. (vv. 2; 6–7)

In recovery, we will pass through many valleys of
tears. Be it tears of frustration, anger, grief, loneliness, or separation, they can become tears of
healing. It seems that tears can wash away years
of poison, cleansing the soul, preparing us for
growth. As addicts/codependents, we were stuck
for so long in the pity-party syndrome that, even
though we may have cried, the tears were not
really healing tears.

In recovery, we experience so many emotions, from deep sorrow to excitement and joy. Before recovery, we had anesthetized our ability to feel because most of what we felt was negative and brought pain. But we can't turn off negative emotions without turning off the positive emotions. As Christians in recovery, we may think it's wrong to feel this or that, but we feel what we feel. How we handle these emotions is what makes them right or wrong. Notice that we are to "pass through" the place of tears—not build a house and live there. Our Father created us as emotional beings, and he can teach us how to handle and express human emotions in a healthy way.

O God, teach me to weep the tears that aid
my recovery.

Psalm
85

Show us your unfailing love, O Lord, and
grant us your salvation. . . .
Love and faithfulness meet together,
righteousness and peace kiss each other.
Faithfulness springs forth from the earth, and
righteousness looks down from heaven.
The Lord will indeed give what is good, and our
land will yield its harvest. (vv. 7; 10–12)

Recovery progresses as those sponsors, loved ones, and friends exhibit "tough love." Often God will love us with that noncompromising love that will not allow us to become sloppy in our recovery. It isn't because he is angry with us but because he knows how easily we excuse the flesh; and recovery is slowed down when we feed our old nature. Our Father wants us to be free, and when we begin self-defeating behaviors, his love confronts us. God's love, though tough, is unfailing even in the midst of our worst pain, in the midst of the most insane craziness we exhibited in addiction/codependency, even in the middle of denial.

His love is his faithfulness demonstrated to us in many ways. One of these is his commitment to our recovery.

Father, help me accept your gift of
unconditional love.

Psalm
86

*Teach me your way, O Lord, and I will walk in
your truth; give me an undivided heart, that
I may fear your name. (v. 11)*

In recovery, some tasks only God can perform;
others we together accomplish, and a few are ours
alone. God cannot do our job of cooperating with
the program. Only we can work the Twelve Steps,
but God alone can give us an undivided heart. As
addicts/codependents we have divided hearts that
always reach for something or someone who will
temporarily cause us to feel better. We get into
relationships or other addictions thinking these
will bring happiness. Only as we become aware
that we cannot unite our hearts, and as we come
to the Mender of Broken Hearts, will the emptiness and longing be eased.

We can bring the brokenness of our lives and
know that he will teach us how to walk in his
truth until our hearts are once more whole.

*Lord, show me when I've stepped out of my
territory into yours.*

Psalm
87

Indeed, of Zion it will be said, "This one and that one were born in her, and the Most High himself will establish her. (v. 5)

To be established by God in a plan of recovery is real security. Yet most of us never realize this security because we stubbornly cling to the old ways, the secure and familiar methods of coping with life; and all the while our lives become more and more unmanageable. *Real* security comes about as we allow what we have been doing to fade away and we begin to rely completely on God. How uncomfortable that will be at first— how frightening. Turning ourselves over to the care of God is a real faith step, but likewise it is a real recovery step. It doesn't matter if this is the first day of recovery or the twenty-fifth year. Step Three must become a daily discipline. As we choose to do this, God will *establish* us as we make a continuing journey of recovery.

God, give me the courage to rely on you when I want to do my own thing.

Psalm
88

*You have taken my companions and loved ones
from me; the darkness is my closest
friend. (v. 18)*

We may blame God, but in reality it was our ad-
diction/codependency that took our companions
and loved ones from us. Our addiction/codepen-
dency became a prison to our bodies, souls, and
spirits, and as we became walled in, those who
mattered became walled out. Our lives were ones
of isolation and aloneness. One by one our signif-
icant people became less and less important.
Darkness became our closest friend because we
could hide from life.

In recovery, we become aware of our need for
companionship, knowing that getting too "lonely"
will set us up to fall again. Recovery means that
the prison doors are open and we can begin to
venture out and rebuild old relationships in a
healthy way and begin new nonaddictive friend-
ships. Recovery dispels the darkness as we learn
how to nurture those in our lives.

*Lord, please begin to remove those walls of
isolation brick by brick.*

Psalm
89

*I will sing of the Lord's great love forever; with
my mouth I will make your faithfulness
known through all generations.
I will declare that your love stands firm forever,
that you established your faithfulness in
heaven itself. (vv. 1–2)*

One way to carry the message of recovery is to
share all of the struggles *and* victories. Another
way is to tell of God's faithfulness. Reaching out
to fellow strugglers by sharing our stories of recovery refreshes our hearts. To remind ourselves
that our Father was faithful even when we
couldn't believe, even when we failed to make
positive steps, not only encourages others; it
builds our faith in God. To realize that we all walk
along similar pathways and share common feelings is helpful. When we are able to be honest
about bad days, others realize that what they experience is a normal part of recovery, and they are
more able to relax.

Listening to others always helps us keep our
bearings. So today look for someone who may be
having a difficult time and reach out to them. It
will strengthen your own personal recovery.

*Lord, give me creative ways of taking the
message of recovery to others.*

Psalm
90

*For a thousand years in your sight are like a
  day that has just gone by, or like a watch
  in the night. . . .*
*Teach us to number our days aright, that we
  may gain a heart of wisdom.*
*Relent, O Lord! How long will it be? Have
  compassion on your servants. (vv. 4; 12–13)*

A child on a family outing often asks, "Are we
nearly there?" "How much longer?"

In recovery, we often forget that we are not
heading toward some goal where, once we have
arrived, we stop working and relax. Recovery is a
daily life-style; even when we have been sober for
several years, we keep working the Steps.

God is not on our timetable, and he doesn't
watch the calendar to see how long it has taken
us to attain a certain plateau. He has all the time
of eternity. If we work the program faithfully *today*, we are recovering. So why worry about the
time frame?

When we remember that today is all we have,
we are able to do whatever assures us of living

sober lives today. When we live one day at a time, we learn to enjoy where we are, to enjoy this day. We stop letting yesterdays or tomorrows steal our todays.

Lord, help me concentrate on today's Steps and not let tomorrow steal today.

Psalm
91

*He will cover you with his feathers, and under
his wings you will find refuge; his
faithfulness will be your shield and
rampart. . . .*
*Because he loves me, says the Lord, I will rescue
him; I will protect him, for he acknowledges
my name. . . .*
*With long life will I satisfy him and show him
my salvation. (vv. 4; 14; 16)*

We must dwell, live, abide, in the shelter of God
and rest in his shadow. He is our only fortress,
our only refuge, and we make the choice to trust.
He will save us from addiction/codependency and
from the aftermath of the destruction of that manner of living. We can take refuge under his wings.
Remembering his faithfulness will shield us. To
live in God—inside God, in Jesus, to really live
there—no harm will destroy us, no disaster. Most
of us think that God is insurance against trouble,
struggles, pain, or disappointment. He is not. But
he does say he will be with us in trouble; he will
hear us when we call on him; and he will show
us his salvation, deliverance, hope, and victory.

*Father, teach me to abide in you during stormy
times as well as sunshiny days.*

Psalm
92

It is good to praise the Lord and make music to
*   your name, O Most High,*
to proclaim your love in the morning and your
*   faithfulness at night. (vv. 1–2)*

Maybe not today, but one day when recovery is
well established we will find it good to praise the
Lord. We will then tell other addicted/codepen-
dent people about the hope of recovery. We will
be able to tell those who have not yet committed
themselves to a program of recovery that God
loves them *as they are.* We will be able to tell others
that he is faithful even in the midnight of our discouragement, that he never leaves or forsakes us
even when we scream at him in our anger. It is
this message that Step Twelve encourages us to
share. We will live to see our enemy—addiction/
codependency—defeated. Our lives will still
count. We shall yet be free—recovery does
happen.

O God, remind me that recovery happens if I
allow it to happen.

Psalm
93

*The Lord reigns, he is robed in majesty; the
Lord is robed in majesty and is armed with
strength. The world is firmly established; it
cannot be moved. (v. 1)*

The Lord reigns! What a statement of recovery. As
long as we try to reign or control, recovery will
not continue. When we allow God to be in charge
and reign over us, then we progressively experience recovery. Sounds so easy, but in reality it is
one of the most difficult tasks in recovery. When
we allow the Lord to reign, we surrender our
wills, our plans, even our lives. To admit we are
powerless is very hard, but to actually resign as
"boss" and allow God to direct is frightening. Yet
peace comes when we *give up.* We may come to a
place of allowing the Lord to reign today, but it is
easy to reclaim our position if we are not careful.
Today the Lord reigns in our recovery. Today we
will experience peace.

*Lord, when I hate to give up, let go, or turn it
over, give me the strength.*

Psalm
94

O Lord, the God who avenges, O God who
avenges, shine forth. . . .
The Lord knows the thoughts of man; he knows
that they are futile. . . .
Unless the Lord had given me help, I would
soon have dwelt in the silence of death.
(vv. 1; 11; 17)

We want God to take vengeance, and we would
certainly enjoy being on the "God squad" when
he does take vengeance on those who have hurt
us. How completely normal to feel this, and yet
while we hold onto those grievances and hope
"they get theirs," we aren't moving forward in our
recovery. Is it worth it?

Stinking thinking is completely futile, and God
is always working to help us see that our *sick
thinking* will keep pulling us back into those old
ways. God wants to teach us how to change those
negative, defeating thought patterns.

Addictions and codependencies are progressive
and terminal diseases. We may not die physically
from codependency for a long time, but we are
not living either. In actuality, we are dead while
we still breathe—a good description of our former
state of addiction/codependency. Recovery assures us that we *live* while we live.

Lord, when I want to have vengeance, help me
to release those who have hurt me.

Psalm
95

Today, if you hear his voice, do not harden your
hearts as you did at Meribah; as you did that
day at Massah in the desert. . . .
For forty years I was angry with that
generation; I said, "They are a people whose
hearts go astray, and they have not known
my ways." (vv. 8; 10)

Addiction/codependency may not literally em-
balm us, but certainly when we are not recovering
we harden our hearts toward God, others, self,
life.

Indeed, our hearts have gone astray as we
search for the next minute of relief. Our hearts
stay astray as long as we refuse to surrender our
lives to God.

We are able to "turn off" our ability to hear
those who are concerned, and we rebelliously follow our own wills. Most of us in recovery found
out that, when we follow our plans, our lives became unmanageable. When we allow God to direct us, we find peace and hope. God will help
our hearts to soften and will teach our hearts to
follow him.

Lord, you are the only one who can manage
my recovery.

Psalm
96

Sing to the Lord, a new song; sing to the Lord,
*   all the earth.*
Sing to the Lord, praise his name; proclaim his
*   salvation day after day. (vv. 1–2)*

Just think! A day will come in recovery when the
darkness will fade into sunrise and joy will come.
We will experience the emotion of joy, and laughter will come where for so long only sadness re-
sided. Praise will come from our mouths, and we
will enjoy sharing our stories of recovery with
others.

Today it may be difficult to think of that ever
happening, but joy is the by-product of recovery.
It just happens! Recovery is a *new song,* and each
one of us writes our own.

Begin to listen and see what the heart is singing, then sing that song over and over until it is a
part of you. Today we may not feel like singing,
but one day soon our songs of recovery will become familiar.

Father, help me look for the sunrise, even on
days when storms rage.

Psalm
97

*All who worship images are put to shame, those
who boast in idols—worship him, all you
gods! . . .
Let those who love the Lord hate evil, for he
guards the lives of his faithful ones and
delivers them from the hand of the wicked.
(vv. 7; 10)*

Addiction is worshiping the chemical; codependency and emotionally dependent relationships
are worshiping the person. Both are idol worship.
We worship the image. We try to connect to the
person and draw our lives from them. In codependent relationships, we enable . . . rescue . . . fix
. . . bail out.

We put our entire lives into these people, sure
that we have enough love to make them well.
Nothing is too much! We don't only go the extra
mile; we travel miles and miles extra. But still we
are just as sick with addiction as the alcoholic or
drug addict. We are addicted to people and
relationships.

For recovery to happen, we must come to the
truth that no human love is enough to bring recovery. When our "savior" complex begins to die,
then recovery will begin.

*O God, help me know the difference between
helping and enabling.*

Psalm
98

Sing to the Lord a new song, for he has done
marvelous things; his right hand and his
holy arm have worked salvation for him.
(v. 1)

Notice that the "joyful psalms" are at the rear of
the book. Thank God! Most of us couldn't be joyful or hopeful at the beginning of our journey—
the pain was too great.

But after several weeks, on some days we actually could feel hopeful in spite of the pain.
Learning how the program works and the con-
cepts of our Twelve-Step living gives us a promise
for the future. Eventually, our emotions begin to
level out and become well enough for us to experience some of the joy of recovery. The best news
of all is that our song in recovery will not be a
slow melancholy tune but will be happy and ju-
bilant. Even if we can't carry a tune, a joyful noise
will emanate from our innermost being.

O God, may my song of recovery begin soon.

Psalm
99

*The Lord reigns, let the nations tremble; he sits
enthroned between the cherubim, let the earth
shake. . . .*
*Exalt the Lord our God and worship at his holy
mountain, for the Lord our God is holy.*
(vv. 1; 9)

"The Lord reigns" is the theme of recovery. If the
Lord is reigning in our lives, it will bring us to
recovery. On the other hand, recovery brings us
to a spiritual awakening, and we want the Lord to
reign. Either way, admitting our powerlessness
over anything or anyone helps us seek his power.

To exalt means that we place something or
someone higher. To recover means we place our
Lord higher than self . . . relationships . . . chem-
icals . . . food . . . sex . . . gambling . . . nicotine.

Recovery is a style of living that constantly ex-
alts God over our lives—a way of life that assures
victory in recovery.

*O God, be exalted over everything and everyone
else in my life.*

Psalm
100

Shout for joy to the Lord, all the earth.
Worship the Lord with gladness, come before
*   him with joyful songs.*
Know that the Lord is God. It is he who made
*   us, and we are his; we are his people, the*
*   sheep of his pasture.*
Enter his gates with thanksgiving and his
*   courts with praise; give thanks to him and*
*   praise his name.*
For the Lord is good and his love endures
*   forever; his faithfulness continues through*
*   all generations. (vv. 1–5)*

As our recovery progresses, we will begin to feel better emotionally, physically, and spiritually. New days begin to be something to look forward to rather than something to endure. As health returns to us, excitement becomes a part of recovery. Gladness, worship, joy, thanksgiving, and praise become real expressions of having had a spiritual awakening—of knowing our God. At some point in our recovery, we began to see God in a different light. Rather than an angry, distant, hard-to-reach, sometimes absent God, we see him as very concerned about us—very present with us, compassionate, and committed to our recovery. How different the relationship, because in recovery we have truly entered into a *living* relationship, and we have continuously improved our knowledge of him through prayer and meditation. Getting well again while getting to know God—what a combination!

Father, knowing you is helping me get well. I want to know you even more.

Psalm 101

I will be careful to lead a blameless life—when will you come to me? I will walk in my house with blameless heart. (v. 2)

Only God can make us blameless by clearing, cleansing, and forgiving us. Most of us as addicts/codependents have a tendency to want to be blameless by blaming someone else or by excusing our behavior. Blaming others has been in effect since the first couple tried to shift the blame for their choices to each other and the serpent. To blame others will not help us to recover; but taking responsibility for our actions and reactions, our behavior and our stinking thinking will promote recovery.

Today we are responsible to walk in the Twelve Steps of recovery. We are responsible for our behavior, our words. *We are responsible*. We didn't cause anyone else to drink, to do drugs, or to be codependent; but *we must face the fact* that we are responsible for *us*.

Father, I need strength to take responsibility for myself.

Psalm
102

Hear my prayer, O Lord; let my cry for help
come to you. . . .
He will respond to the prayer of the destitute; he
will not despise their plea. . . .
In the course of my life he broke my strength;
he cut short my days. (vv. 1; 17; 23)

God does respond to the prayer of the destitute.
As addicts/codependents, we had reached the
depths of destitution before we were able to call
on the Lord. Because of our false pride, it was
most difficult to admit that we needed any help,
and even more humbling to ask for assistance. As
long as we think we can handle our lives, we will
continue to struggle in our own puny, weak
"strength" against a giant that is much too strong
for us.

It is good news to realize that God does not
despise our plea. Because he wants us whole, he
waits patiently for our own efforts to wear thin so
we can come to the real source of recovery. God's
"severe mercy" breaks our strength so he can cut
short our days of addiction/codependency. Sometimes it's difficult for us to be grateful that God

helps the bottom come up to meet us rather than waiting for us to "bottom out." In this sense, we can actually become thankful for the pain of destitution that brought us to recovery.

O God, thank you for bringing the bottom up to meet me and for the recovery that began in my life.

Psalm
103

*Praise the Lord, O my soul; and forget not all
his benefits—who forgives all your sins and
heals all your diseases, who redeems your
life from the pit and crowns you with love
and compassion. (vv. 2–4)*

What a beautiful promise to those of us who have
suffered dependency of any kind. He forgives all
the messes we have made, and he heals all our
diseases—even the disease of addiction/codependency. Then, to top it off, he redeems our lives
from destruction.

Truly, we who struggle against addiction/codependency are oppressed. But take heart, God isn't
mad at us; he never treats us like we deserve to
be treated. Rather he loves us like a good daddy
or mommy loves a dependent child.

In recovery, treatment is the beginning; but recovery is a day-by-day choice that we make to
work our program and depend totally on God. We
take responsibility for our actions and words and
live in a manner consistent with our plan of
recovery.

*O God, help me make the day-by-day choice to
work my program while depending on you.*

Psalm
104

*Praise the Lord, O my soul. O Lord my God,
you are very great; you are clothed with
splendor and majesty. (v. 1)*

A power greater than ourselves! This psalm describes how great our God is. Surely a God who has the power to do all that he has done (listed in the entirety of this psalm) can handle our recovery. The God who created all of this world, who created water and designed its boundaries, can surely handle our grief—the sorrow, the tears of recovery.

Is there any doubt that he can handle our anger and confusion? God understands the emotions of our humanness, and he can teach us how to process all of those emotions in such a way as to further our recovery. *God is big enough* to direct our plan of recovery and faithful enough never to abandon us—no matter what we may feel.

*Lord, please reassure me often that I am not
alone on this journey.*

Psalm
105

*Glory in his name; let the hearts of those who
seek the Lord rejoice. (v. 3)*

Recovery happens—but it will not happen alone.
We need God, and we need others. We need to
find that place in him so that we can run and hide
on days when discouragement overtakes us. We
need others to listen to us and give us insight and
encouragement.

We need to be able to rejoice in his presence
over the daily victories—as a child who has made
an accomplishment or passed a test. We need others who can applaud our milestones in recovery.
So our relationship with our Father God and our
support groups go hand-in-hand to continue our
recovery. The two together assure us that we will
make it; trying to do it without one or the other
makes recovery difficult and doubtful. *We need
God, and we need others.*

Many times we ask our Father for things we are
sure we need or want. We all think we know what
is best for us. We tell God what we need and want
and tell him how to run our recovery, forgetting
that he knows what we need. We ask for pain or
trouble removed, and yet it is precisely this pain
or trouble that brought us to recovery. Being the

humans we are, instant release from pain and pressure would make us less diligent to pursue our program of recovery.

He gives us *what we need* exactly—like a parent who feeds green beans when the child wants jelly beans. But we fail to see how he is caring for us, even in this present circumstance.

Lord, remind me that you give what I need to further my journey of recovery.

Psalm
106

Who can proclaim the mighty acts of the Lord
or fully declare his praise? . . .
We have sinned, even as our fathers did; we
have done wrong and acted wickedly. . . .
Yet he saved them for his name's sake, to make
his mighty power known. . . .
But they soon forgot what he had done and did
not wait for his counsel. (vv. 2; 6; 8; 13)

Who can proclaim the mighty acts of the Lord any
better than those of us who are actively recovering? Who can take the message of God's help in
recovery, his willingness to meet us at the point
of our need? We who have been there!

It's good news to realize that, even though we
have blown it, he has not ceased caring for us,
loving us, and making a way for us. *God is so faithful.* Thank goodness that his love for us does not
hinge on our ability to be good, to perform.

How soon we tend to forget what he has done,
and then we find ourselves trying to run our lives,
to take charge, to manage our lives. Once more
our lives become unmanageable, and we find ourselves having to go back to the first three Steps.

Those first three Steps were our salvation then,
and they will once again set us on the road to
recovery.

God, I want to thank you for having never
given up on me.

Psalm
107

Let the redeemed of the Lord say this—those he
*   redeemed from the hand of the foe. . . .*
Then they cried to the Lord in their trouble, and
*   he saved them from their distress. . . .*
Whoever is wise, let him heed these things and
*   consider the great love of the Lord.*
*   (vv. 2; 13; 43)*

In our twelfth Step, we find one of the most sat-
isfying parts of recovery: being able to encourage
someone else to begin recovery. We have been delivered from the hand of the enemy, and God can
help others. Sharing our stories, being available to
go to someone else with the message that God is
the God of recovery, gives support to someone
who is having a bad day.

In this psalm, we see several different sets of
circumstances that result in people calling out for
God's help. We may have wandered in a desert of
our own choosing that left us hungry, thirsty, our
lives ebbing slowly away. No one could help—and
then in that desperation we turned to the Lord.
We cried out, and he heard us; but more than just
hearing, he began to deliver us from distress.
Each one of us got to the end of our rope in a
different way, but when we cried out, he respond-
ed and helped.

Lord, thank you for bringing me to the end of
my rope.

Psalm
108

Give us aid against the enemy, for the help of
man is worthless.
With God we will gain the victory, and he will
trample down our enemies. (vv. 12–13)

Addiction/codependency is a disease. True, had
we not ever sampled the first drink, cigarette,
drug, pie, or person, we might not have ever
experienced the depth of despair that addiction/
codependency brings. Yet even in our worst mess,
God wants to reach out to us. Only God can
deliver us.

We are not the enemy; they are not the enemy.
Addiction/codependency is the enemy.

But many times we turn on ourselves, we turn
on each other, thinking we're attacking the enemy.
Only when we properly define the enemy and begin fighting that real enemy, only when our
thoughts and energies are turned to fighting—not
people—but a lifestyle of death, can we experience victory.

Lord, help me define the real enemy.

Psalm
109

*But you, O Sovereign Lord, deal well with me
for your name's sake; out of the goodness of
your love, deliver me.
For I am poor and needy, and my heart is
wounded within me. . . .
For he stands at the right hand of the needy
one, to save his life from those who
condemn him. (vv. 21–22; 31)*

Addiction/codependency indeed leave mortal
wounds within us and in the hearts of those around
us. The wounds become even more infected when
we neglect them by living in denial or avoidance.
Family members also bear wounds because the disease and its effect on us has stolen many precious
times. There are many broken promises. The disease is the enemy! Now is the time to recover these
losses by making amends where possible, making
restitution where the opportunity presents itself.
Now is the time to rebuild relationships, to express the
deep feelings of love and appreciation that we have
neglected to verbalize. Recovery sets us free to in-
vest our lives in a better direction.

*Lord, show me how to make restitution and
rebuild relationships.*

Psalm
110

*The Lord says to my Lord: "Sit at my right
hand until I make your enemies a footstool
for your feet." (v. 1)*

Which enemies was David speaking about? Those
who chased him and sought to take his life. Our
enemies of addiction/codependency have given
hot pursuit. Had we not entered the safety of recovery, those enemies would have stolen our
lives, joy, peace, health, and relationships.

Staying close to the Lord of recovery assures us
that we can be triumphant over these enemies. So
we just sit at his right hand by meditating on his
goodness, forgiveness, mercy, patience, love, and
compassion. As we sit in his presence and become
more secure with him, we will begin to hear the
healing Word that our Father is speaking to us.
As we hear that healing Word, our spirits are
strengthened to continue the battle. If we're failing in recovery, it's because we have been fighting
in our *own* strength.

*O God, help me realize that failure to recover is
the result of depending on myself.*

Psalm
111

Praise the Lord. I will extol the Lord with all
my heart in the counsel of the upright and in
the assembly.
Great are the works of the Lord; they are
pondered by all who delight in them.
(vv. 1–2)

Those of us who have been in the depths of ad-
diction/codependency and are now in the process
of recovery cannot help but praise the Lord. We
remember from where we came. With grateful
hearts we share with others our stories, our lives,
and now our hope. Remembering the past no
longer sends us tumbling into the abyss but rather
reminds us that God has faithfully brought us
miles and miles in recovery. We are a demonstra-
tion to others of God's faithfulness to those who
desire recovery. One method of praise is to share
our stories; another is to lift our hearts and voices
and tell God how much we appreciate and thank
him for recovery.

Lord, "thank you" seems so small in
comparison to your great gift of recovery.

Psalm
112

*Surely he will never be shaken; a righteous man
  will be remembered forever.
He will have no fear of bad news; his heart is
  steadfast, trusting in the Lord.
His heart is secure, he will have no fear; in the
  end he will look in triumph on his foes.
  (vv. 6–8)*

Recovery brings our heavenly Father into focus.
As we begin to recover, we begin to see him as
our friend and not an enemy. We begin to understand that what we previously thought was freedom (doing our own thing) actually took us into
deep bondage. Only as we acknowledged our inability to run our own lives did we begin to come
out of that terrible captivity. Our hearts became
more secure with God. Even when bad news
comes to us, we are able to remain steadfast because we trust the Lord.

We will look back over our lives and realize that
addiction/codependency is defeated on a daily basis as we are faithful to work our program and
look to God.

Father, you refocus life and help me see clearly.

Psalm
113

He raises the poor from the dust and lifts the
needy from the ash heap;
he seats them with princes, with the princes of
their people. (vv. 7–8)

If we allow him, God can give us peace and sat-
isfaction no matter what we face in recovery.
Every day is not a joyful day—that is life and that
is reality. But joy does come again. Just think,
even our bad days are not as bad as our good days
before we began to recover. Now we are able to
remember that this day is going to pass—and
with it the emotions. Another reason to praise the
Lord!

Before recovery, bad days were the only way it
could be. Our God stoops down and raises the
addicted/codependent from the depths of addiction; he takes us from the ash heap of destruction,
gives us dignity as people, and restores our self-
worth and identity. He displays us because he is
delighted that we are his children. We belong!

O God, you have given back the dignity and
self-worth my addiction had stolen.

Psalm
114

*When Israel came out of Egypt, the house of
Jacob from a people of foreign tongue,
Judah became God's sanctuary, Israel his
dominion. (vv. 1–2)*

Coming out of Egypt is the same as our coming
out of the bondage of addiction/codependency.
God did not lead the children of Israel by the
shortest, most economical route. He took them
the long way home. And so it is in our recovery.
He knows that we learn great lessons about ourselves, life, others, and God when we aren't instantly delivered. Our faith matures as we
experience those most difficult of times and find
our Father still present. Our faith muscles build
as we depend on him over and over. The lessons
of powerlessness are taught again and again as we
temporarily try our wings and fail. Problems in
relationships and finances give us more oppor-
tunities to continue taking our personal inventories. So maybe the long road to recovery is an
asset after all.

Thank you, God, for the slowness of recovery.

*O God, strengthen me as you lead me the "long
way" home.*

Psalm
115

May the Lord make you increase, both you and
your children.
May you be blessed by the Lord, the Maker of
heaven and earth. (vv. 14–15)

Addiction/codependency has subtracted not only
from us personally; our families have also suffered. But recovery brings us into a place with our
Father where he begins to increase, and that
blessing of increase overflows to our loved ones.
One thing that was lost in our days of addiction/
codependency was trust, confidence, and reliabil-
ity. We were too sick to hold fast to our word. We
meant well, but something always interfered. But
as recovery continues, we are once more able to
do what we say we will do. Therefore, our family's ability to trust us increases. This is a wonderful benefit of recovery. Our health improves—our
attitude becomes more positive. The blessings of
recovery touch not only the addict/codependent
but also our children and other family members.

Father, I am so glad you can redeem all that
addiction has taken.

Psalm
116

*For you, O Lord, have delivered my soul from
death, my eyes from tears, my feet from
stumbling, that I may walk before the Lord in
the land of the living. (vv. 8–9)*

Addiction/codependency means three things: tears,
stumbling, and death. That is the progression of
our disease, and outside of recovery there is no
hope. Giving up all hope that we will ever be able
to turn this around, we cried in desperation to the
Lord. At the point of our greatest need, God
stepped in and delivered our souls from death, our
eyes from tears, and finally our feet from stumbling.
The end result is that we can walk before the Lord
in the land of the living. It is easy to love the Lord
because we who are in recovery are well aware that
without him there would be no recovery. He heard
us then, and he hears us now. We are encouraged
to call on him daily for as long as we live. He will
always be there.

*Lord, teach me that you have always been
available and you always will be.*

Psalm
117

For great is his love toward us, and the
faithfulness of the Lord endures forever. (v. 2)

Great is his love toward us

- when we are doing well in recovery,
- when we are struggling,
- when we feel loved,
- when we feel abandoned,
- when we believe,
- when we don't believe.

God's love doesn't depend on how well we have done spiritually. It isn't contingent on what we feel emotionally. His love doesn't rely on how many steps we have accomplished this week in recovery. *His love is a gift to us,* even on the days we deserve it least. God's love is unconditional—there are no strings and not one "I love you if . . ."

Even when we don't receive his love, it doesn't stop. If we run away, his love continues to reach out and search for us.

God's love is demonstrated to us over and over again, especially in his faithfulness never to abandon us and never to give up on us.

O God, thank you for loving me no
matter what.

Psalm
118

I was pushed back and about to fall, but the
Lord helped me.
The Lord is my strength and my song; he has
become my salvation. (vv. 13–14)

Relapse in recovery is common unless we continue to work the program and take the Steps. Many
people think they are recovering because they are
no longer using, but in reality they are not living
sober lives. Anytime we forget that God is the
source of our sobriety, we are headed for a fall.
Any day we stop taking a personal inventory, we
are backing up. If we cease improving our awareness of God, that will cause us to fall.

Recovery is growth, and unless we are growing
in each of the Steps, we begin to lose ground.
Even in times of danger—when we are facing or
experiencing relapse—God helps us. He is our
strength, and he can turn our relapses around if
only we will once more come to him and allow
him to be our salvation.

O God, help me to grow and mature in
recovery—day by day.

Psalm
119

Your word is a lamp to my feet and a light for
my path. (v. 105)

God's Word is essential to our continuing recovery. As Christians in recovery, our spirits and souls need the food that his Word gives. God's Word becomes food when we are starving. It is a light that shines on the pathway of recovery. God's Word is a lamp to our journey. In fact, the Word is the map to whatever destination we have in life.

Many times the enemy beats us with the Word, and we think it's the way our Father feels about us. When the Word brings fear or anxiety, it's time to remind ourselves that God's Word

- encourages,
- strengthens,
- edifies,
- comforts,
- heals,
- delivers.

God corrects with such gentle pressure and loving concern that we quickly want to repent, and hope surrounds us. Don't be afraid to hear our Father's Word today.

Lord, draw me deeper into your Word.

Psalm
120

I call on the Lord in my distress, and he
answers me.
Save me, O Lord, from lying lips and from
deceitful tongues. (vv. 1–2)

Distress is often the by-product of our own stinking thinking and negative attitudes. Save us,
Lord, from our lying lips and deceitful tongues.
Without even realizing it, many times we talk ourselves into distress and discouragement without
ever opening our mouths. What we meditate on—
the thoughts we entertain, the memories we re-
hearse—all has an effect on what we feel. In recovery, we have a tendency to look back at our
failures, and that causes us distress, unless we are
able to also see those failures as instruments that
brought us to recovery. Many times we view ourselves the way we were and forget that we are still
becoming. When we look back, we must always remember to mingle in with the memory the positive, the progress, the Steps we've made. What
was is in the past. What we are *now* is important.
But what we are going to be gives hope!

O God, keep my eyes fixed on the goal
of recovery.

Psalm
121

I lift up my eyes to the hills—where does my
help come from?
My help comes from the Lord, the Maker of
heaven and earth.
He will not let your foot slip—he who watches
over you will not slumber. (vv. 1–3)

From where does our help come? Only the God of recovery can go through each weary day, over every mountain that seems much too steep, and into those sleepless nights with us. Friends grow weary; loved ones can't always be there; even members of our support groups may not always be available. But God will always be there! He will keep us from slipping back into old habits. Every day of recovery God is standing there wanting to help, yet many times we miss that fact because of our pain or because he doesn't do it our way or because we can't feel him.

Nonetheless, God is a very present help in our journey of recovery.

O God, never let me forget that you are
always present.

Psalm
122

*I rejoiced with those who said to me, "Let us go
to the house of the Lord." (v. 1)*

Improving our conscious contact with God is
greatly helped by fellowshipping with our brothers and sisters. In the first stage of recovery, we
may have avoided going to church because we
were ashamed or in too much pain or it was just
too much trouble. But as recovery has progressed
past those days, we need that support also.
Christians sometimes have a tendency to be in-
sensitive to others who are hurting. But never let
that be said of us in recovery. We never know
what may be going on in the heart of the person
sitting across from us. Just a smile or an encour-
aging word may give someone else the courage
they need to face their struggle. So going to
church can be a twofold blessing. Our spirits can
be fed as we listen, and then we may be a blessing
to someone else.

*Lord, direct my steps to the place of worship
where I need to be.*

Psalm
123

Have mercy on us, O Lord, have mercy on us,
for we have endured much contempt.
We have endured much ridicule from the proud,
much contempt from the arrogant. (vv. 3–4)

As addicts/codependents we have experienced a good bit of contempt and ridicule from others. But the biggest source of ridicule and contempt is not from outside of ourselves but from within. We belittle ourselves, tear ourselves down, criticize and hate ourselves. Our low self-worth comes not nearly so much from what others think and say as from what we say and think. We speak very hurtful things in our hearts all day long; we call ourselves names and then wonder why we have not been successful in life. The approval we need the most is not that of our friend, our spouse, our parent or child . . . *it is our own.* Until we can accept the person that we are and love that person and affirm that person, no one else can make a difference. Even God's healing words will not help. Today we need most of all to accept who we are.

O God, give me the ability to accept myself and
appreciate what you are making me.

Psalm
124

We have escaped like a bird out of the fowler's
snare; the snare has been broken, and we
have escaped.
Our help is in the name of the Lord, the
Maker of heaven and earth. (vv. 7–8)

Only those who have lived in the snare of addiction/codependency know how powerful that prison is. Only we who have escaped through recovery know the wonderful freedom that God has brought to us.

In the disease, the more we struggled, the more entangled we became. The more we fought, the weaker we got. But when we were truly able to realize that our only help was in a Power greater than ourselves and we turned wholeheartedly to God, *then* the snare was broken. In the beginning, our help was in the Lord, but also our continuing help each day is in the Lord. He is still the only one who can keep us free. The potential is there. Sometimes we are ready to fall. But if we will remind ourselves that our help is in the Lord and call to him, he will keep us out of the snare of the fowler.

O God, protect me from the snare of addiction.

Psalm
125

*Those who trust in the Lord are like Mount
Zion, which cannot be shaken but endures
forever. (v. 1)*

What a simple statement: Those who trust in the
Lord cannot be shaken but endure forever. But
what a powerful statement: *Trust in the Lord.* What
a way to declare our powerlessness, our confidence that he can restore us and turn our wills
and lives over to God. Search our hearts. Confess
to God. Allow God to remove defects. Make restitution. Continue to understand ourselves. Improve conscious contact with God, praying for
power to carry out his will. Tell others.

Trusting in the Lord assures us that, as long as
we are trusting, we cannot be shaken. No storm,
no trouble, no failure can defeat us because we
are trusting in the Lord.

*O God, help me know that I can trust you
through whatever I face.*

Psalm
126

When the Lord brought back the captives to
*   Zion, we were like men who dreamed.*
Our mouths were filled with laughter, our
*   tongues with songs of joy.*
Then it was said among the nations, "The Lord
*   has done great things for them." (vv. 1–3)*

When we who were captive were given freedom
and were able to enjoy the fruit of recovery, it was
a dream come true. After the tears of guilt,
shame, repentance, and grief were shed, laughter
began to be part of our recovery. To laugh is to
lift our spirits—to sing lifts them even higher. To
those of us in recovery, there is much to laugh
about, and to have a sense of humor is a great
asset. Laughter does good like a medicine, especially when we learn to laugh at ourselves. Indeed, the Lord has done great things for us, and
when we are truly aware of how much he has
done, songs of joy will come naturally. Even if you
can't carry a tune, a joyful noise will come forth.

O God, help me laugh my way through the
difficult as well as the humorous events.

Psalm
127

*Unless the Lord builds the house, its builders
labor in vain. Unless the Lord watches over
the city, the watchmen stand guard in
vain. (v. 1)*

Back to square (Step) One! Humans that we are,
we must continually be reminded that our lives,
our plans, our biggest efforts cannot make us
whole. Until we give up the struggle and make a
decision to turn our lives and wills over to God,
recovery will be, at best, a rocky road.

Recovery is a continual refresher course on our
powerlessness and our need to turn our lives over
to the care of God. How faithful he is to remind
us through daily circumstances, his Word, and
the Twelve Steps that we must have God as the
center of our recovery.

*O God, remind me that you are the center of
my recovery.*

Psalm
128

Blessed are all who fear the Lord, who walk in
his ways.
You will eat the fruit of your labor; blessings
and prosperity will be yours. (vv. 1–2)

Walking in the ways of God brings blessings into our lives. Depending on him, turning our lives and wills over to God, brings us to a place of trust and rest. Peace in our hearts is the by-product, the fruit of recovery. We cannot make anyone else in our lives recover, but we can continue to work on our own recovery. We can continue to walk in the pathway of recovery. Many times the changes that occur in an individual's recovery evoke changes in those around them. That is sometimes the fruit of recovery.

The best fruit that our sobriety produces is spiritual, physical, and emotional well-being. Regardless of what else happens, recovery leaves us much better than when we were struggling alone. Everyone profits when we continue the journey.

O God, thank you for the many fruits
of recovery.

Psalm
129

*They have greatly oppressed me from my
youth, but they have not gained the victory
over me. . . .*
*But the Lord is righteous; he has cut me free
from the cords of the wicked. (vv. 2; 4)*

For many of us, addiction did not begin the day
we took the first drink, used the first drug, or felt
the first emotional high resulting from a codependent relationship. Our addiction/codependency
may have begun years before. Part of the emotional side of addiction/codependency is the fact
that we never learned how to handle pain, problems, or emotions. So we repressed them, creat-
ing a volcano inside that was ready to erupt.
When the emotions became so uncomfortable we
could not stand it, we began to look for something
or someone to ease the pain. It is especially difficult for adult children of alcoholic/dysfunctional
homes to know that it is even all right to *feel*. Recovery brings us to an awareness that God understands our emotions and will help us deal with
them appropriately. Emotions are neither right
nor wrong. What matters is how we handle them.

*Lord, I need your assistance in handling
my emotions.*

Psalm
130

If you, O Lord, kept a record of sins, O Lord,
*   who could stand?*
But with you there is forgiveness; therefore you
*   are feared. . . .*
For with the Lord is unfailing love and with
*   him is full redemption. (vv. 3–4; 7)*

Steps Four and Five are frightening when we realize that we can no longer hide from ourselves
what has always been known by God. To see what
we have done, to realize who we have hurt, to see
the debris we have left behind is overwhelming.
To have to face this with God would be overwhelming unless we were aware that there is forgiveness for each deed and each failure. We are
released from the guilt as we begin to add Steps
Eight and Nine to the procedure. Although these
Steps can be the most difficult of all, there will be
such freedom and healing as we humble ourselves
and make restitution. To have God forgive us is
paramount, but the completion of that act is to
acknowledge to another human our sin and failure and then make amends where possible. God
will give us grace to do this very difficult task of
recovery.

God, give me the grace to share my inventory
with someone else.

Psalm
131

But I have stilled and quieted my soul; like a
weaned child with its mother, like a weaned
child is my soul within me. (v. 2)

This was the promise God gave us personally when we began our journey into recovery. Although the journey never ends, we progress along, finding much of the anxiety, fear, turmoil, and frustration of letting go of something or someone that eased our pain. We also find peace and quietness filling the void.

Weaning children is very difficult, and little ones fuss and complain and cry. But after awhile, it begins to happen. The baby finds new ways of going to sleep, finds something else to pacify itself. Nursing becomes a thing of the past, and joy in this new developmental stage replaces the joy the child once knew with mother.

One day we will be like a child who is weaned; our souls will be quiet and still, and we will know peace.

O Lord, fill with peace the void left
by addiction.

Psalm
132

O Lord, remember David and all the hardships
he endured. (v. 1)

By changing one word in this verse, we can enter
into our own personal pity party. By putting our
names where David's is, we can begin to recount
all of the hardships we have endured. We can
whine and complain and maybe even find someone else who will listen, since a pity party without
guests is quite boring. The more we remember the
hardships, with a "poor us" attitude, the worse
we will feel. So why not turn the pity party
around and begin to see instead how those hardships paved the way for recovery. When we become grateful for things that have happened in
the past, we have taken a giant step toward
recovery.

A grateful heart is never out of style. Remember
the hardship, of course, but with a positive
outlook.

O God, help me to have a positive and hopeful
outlook when I remember the hardships that
brought me to recovery.

Psalm
133

How good and pleasant it is when brothers live
together in unity! (v. 1)

Unity is the entire theme of recovery, the wholeness of body, spirit, and soul. When we are
whole, then we experience personal unity—peace
within.

Since we no longer try to control other people,
circumstances, or events, we can spend that time
bringing about unity in our own lives. Then we
can pray that others in our lives and families will
also begin and maintain a recovery in their own
lives. Regardless of what others do, we can keep
working our program, taking appropriate steps of
recovery. Remembering that after the pain is acknowledged, rather than hidden, wholeness
comes. And with wholeness comes unity.

Personal unity is often easier to attain than unity with others. But often when we have laid aside
our grievances, forgiven others, and given our
lives and wills over to God, we no longer have the
need to get even. Therefore we may even experience unity in relationships. God is the author of
unity, and he knows what needs to happen in
each life for unity to happen in us.

O God of unity, I ask you to unify all that is
fragmented in my life.

Psalm
134

May the Lord, the Maker of heaven and earth,
bless you from Zion. (v. 3)

May God bless you! Whether recovery has barely begun or we have been on the journey for a long time, may God bless us.

May his blessings be ours on days when victory over some habit, attitude, or problem is imminent—as well as on those days we are sure it will never come.

May God bless us on beautiful, clear, sunshiny days when our hearts are light but also on days when the clouds seem to hide the sunshine. May he bless us!

May God bless us as we live our new lives to the fullest—as we learn to enjoy sober living.

May God bless us whether we are close to home or must travel far away.

May God bless us with recovery, health, contentment, serenity, hope, trust, faith, love—himself!

God, you are the author of blessing, and I thank
you for blessings too numerous to count.

Psalm
135

Praise the Lord. Praise the name of the Lord;
praise him, you servants of the Lord. . . .
Praise be to the Lord from Zion, to him who
dwells in Jerusalem. Praise the Lord.
(vv. 1; 21)

Praise comes from the grateful heart as a natural happening. Praise comes easily when life feels comfortable; praise is not difficult when we feel like it.

But praise can come from our hearts when things aren't going so well for us. This is praise by an act of our wills. This praise is an act of obedience when we'd rather grumble or feel sorry for ourselves. Praise can come from us in the most difficult, painful, and disappointing circumstances—this becomes a sacrifice of praise.

Even on bad days, we can praise God that it won't always be this way, things will get better. To praise our God gets us to focus on something and someone other than ourselves. If today is a good day—praise the Lord! If today is not a good day—praise the Lord out of our brokenness. But whatever we do, praise the Lord.

Father, please help me be willing to make a
sacrifice of praise.

Psalm
136

Give thanks to the Lord, for he is good.
  His love endures forever. . . .
[He] freed us from our enemies, his love endures
  forever. (vv. 1; 24)

Once more an entire story is contained in a few
lines, but each line declares over and over, "His
love endures forever." Every story of recovery is
another declaration that his love does indeed endure forever. That is why taking the message to
others is so important to our recovery. Maybe that
is why the encouragement to share our story is
included in the Twelve Steps.

When we look back and see the hand of God
each step of the way, it reinforces our trust and
faith in our God. Each day we can look back and
be thankful that God, with our cooperation, has
kept us sober. Each story of recovery continues to
make bold statements of God's love, which endures forever. From the story of Creation to the
story we are now living day-by-day, his mercy
does endure forever.

O God, may I never forget your love
and mercy.

Psalm
137

By the rivers of Babylon we sat and wept when
we remembered Zion. (v. 1)

Looking back over a lifetime of wasted years is
certainly reason to weep. Seeing the debris that
we left behind us will steal the joy and rob us of
our song. Yet looking back is sometimes a good
measuring stick to determine our personal growth
in recovery. Looking back can also keep us up to
date on that personal inventory as we see those
areas of failure, as we remember those we have
hurt.

Have we discussed these with our sponsors and
God? Did we make amends to those involved?
Have we forgiven ourselves and others? Have we
received God's forgiveness? Looking back can be
profitable if we allow it. Looking back can give us
new songs as we rejoice because of the rescue
through recovery.

Looking back can give us one more reason to
praise God.

Lord, help me see with realistic vision the
distance you have brought me in recovery.

Psalm
138

I will praise you, O Lord, with all my heart;
  before the "gods" I will sing your
  praise. . . .
When I called, you answered me; you made me
  bold and stouthearted. (vv. 1; 3)

In the early days of our recovery, we had to concentrate on the difficult task of living through a day without drinking, drugging, or running to our co-dependent relationship. After several months, we were able to focus on other things, other people, God, and life. So praise has become possible for us. If the word *praise* seems a little "churchy," try the idea of thanking the Lord. That is what praise is, after all. Praise God—thank God.

One of the areas of praise can always be that, when we called to God, he answered us. He began the work within each one of us to make us bold and stouthearted. This boldness and stoutheartedness comes not from our own strength but because we depend totally on God. Today we can thank him that he has entered into our weakness and has become our strength.

Father, remind me that my weakness gives your
  strength an opportunity to be proven.

Psalm
139

*O Lord, you have searched me and you
know me. . . .
Where can I go from your spirit? Where can I
flee from your presence? . . .
See if there is any offensive way in me, and lead
me in the way everlasting. (vv. 1; 7; 24)*

God knows us. We cannot surprise him. Nothing
we have done or will do will catch him off guard.
He knows our addictive/codependent nature, and
he hates what it has done to us. He is touched by
our struggle, and he has committed himself to our
wholeness—just as much as he was committed to
delivering the children of Israel from Egypt.

Even before recovery, he was there; even when
we were so bound up in addiction/codependency,
he was there. Even when our lives were completely unmanageable and we were so "crazy" that we
didn't want him—still he was there!

He never let go of us. Even the darkness within
our own soul does not frighten him because he
looks through it and sees us. He is leading us in
the "way everlasting," which is more commonly
referred to as recovery.

*Lord, thank you for knowing me and for
continuing to love me anyway.*

Psalm
140

*Rescue me, O Lord, from evil men; protect me
   from men of violence,
who devise evil plans in their hearts and stir up
   war every day. (vv. 1–2)*

When we look outside of ourselves and want God
to get "them," we have lost touch with the truth
of recovery. It is not them we need to worry
about; it is that human, carnal, old nature we still
battle against. It is our hearts that will devise evil
plans to sabotage our recovery. That old nature
will gravitate back to the old thinking, the old attitude, the old playmates and playgrounds. The
evil that is devised is within our own hearts and
will hinder us and always remind us that we're
too busy to spend time with God, that meetings
are boring, that so-and-so talks too much; we
don't need the Twelve Steps.

   Oh, God, rescue us from ourselves and keep us
from falling. Recovery is too precious to lose now.

*O God, keep me in touch with the evil within
myself that is waiting to sabotage my recovery.*

Psalm
141

Set a guard over my mouth, O Lord; keep
watch over the door of my lips. (v. 3)

What a prayer for the recovering person. If anyone needed to have a guard over their mouths, it
is those who have come this far in our journey,
and we forget to speak good things, positive
things, hopeful things.

What we say has a great deal to do with what
we feel. The words we think and the words we
verbalize contribute to our daily emotional well-
being or lack of well-being.

Take a quick inventory—in the last week, what
kind of thoughts and conversation have we been
involved in

- with family members?
- with support group members?
- with friends?
- about recovery?
- about problems?
- about self?
- about life?

Maybe we need to change the prayer to, "Set a
guard over our minds and keep watch over the
doors of our thoughts."

O Lord, help me clean up my thoughts and
guard my words.

Psalm
142

When my spirit grows faint within me, it is
you who know my way. In the path where I
walk men have hidden a snare for me.
Look to my right and see; no one is concerned
for me. I have no refuge; no one cares for my
life.
I cry to you, O Lord; I say, "You are my refuge,
my portion in the land of the living."
(vv. 3–5)

Does it surprise us when we're this far into recovery to find that we still experience days when our spirits grow faint? Are we dismayed to find that everyone isn't excited about our recovery, meetings, Steps, and God? Does it cause us to fall by the wayside when something trips us and we fall? When we try to run back to something comfortable and it no longer feels secure, are we disappointed? We will fail; others will fail. But the good news is that God knows where we are walking, and he doesn't lose sight of us for even a minute. Though no one else is concerned or offers a refuge, *God does care*, and he is our refuge.

Life is full of disappointment and problems, and recovery does not change that. But recovery does equip us to deal with life in a more mature way.

Father, give strength to my spirit to deal with
life more maturely.

Psalm
143

*I remember the days of long ago; I meditate on
all your works and consider what your hands
have done.
I spread out my hands to you; my soul thirsts
for you like a parched land. (vv. 5–6)*

To remember what our lives were like before recovery can be painful, but to add the words of
God in our lives makes it positive. Just to think
about where we have been brings us down, but
to see where we were going gives hope. So always
combine the two: what we are and what God is
making us; where we were and where God is taking us; before recovery and on the journey of
recovery.

As we grow in our recovery, our souls become
thirsty for more of God, reaching out to him as a
child asks for water on a summer day. As we remind ourselves of God's works in our lives, how
can we not want to know him more? After all,
look from where he rescued us!

*O God, knowing you causes me to want to
know you more.*

Psalm
144

Praise be to the Lord my Rock, who trains my
*   hands for war, my fingers for battle.*
He is my loving God and my fortress, my
*   stronghold and my deliverer, my shield, in*
*   whom I take refuge, who subdues peoples*
*   under me. (vv. 1–2)*

The God of recovery, the God of new beginnings,
the God of our lives—and what a God he is!
When we are unstable, he becomes our rock.
When we are defeated in the war, he teaches us
how to do battle. When we are exposed to those
who want to wound us, he surrounds us within
the fortress of himself. A stronghold, a deliverer,
a shield in whom we can hide. Yet he is a God
who helps us turn around and face our greatest
enemy—ourselves.

He is a God who can be depended upon no
matter what is going on in our lives. The God of
recovery is our true friend.

Lord, let me turn to you as my best friend.

Psalm
145

The Lord is gracious and compassionate, slow to
anger and rich in love.
The Lord is good to all; he has compassion on
all he has made. (vv. 8–9)

Many times our idea of God is distorted by wrong
belief, and often that perception hinders our having a good relationship with him. As we seek to
improve our conscious contact, we have two possibilities. We can meditate on what we thought
God was, or we can meditate on what he tells us
about himself.

In this psalm, we see that he is good, righteous,
gracious, compassionate, slow to anger, rich in
love, good to all.

Stop and think: with which God would we find
it easier to build a close relationship? Since our
meditation builds our trust or destroys it, we can
see how important our perception is.

Lord, give us a true knowledge of you.

O God, help me meditate daily on what you tell
me about yourself.

Psalm
146

Do not put your trust in princes, in mortal
men, who cannot save. . . .
Blessed is he whose help is the God of Jacob,
whose hope is in the Lord his God. (vv. 3; 5)

We codependents find it most difficult to turn our
attention away from "mortal men." We addicts
find it more difficult to stop expecting others to
take responsibility for us. But true recovery will
bring each of us to these points of awareness soon
enough.

No one, regardless of how much they love or
care about us, can guarantee to always be there.
No one can save us from addiction/codependency;
no one can walk the road of recovery with us.
This forces us to look to God for our help. God
will not fail—he remains faithful, sets prisoners
free, encourages us when we are down, and will
always walk with us. He is our guarantee of
recovery.

O God, help me stay on track knowing that a
mere human will fail me.

Psalm
147

He heals the brokenhearted and binds up their wounds. (v. 3)

Many of us have experienced desperate wounding that left us with broken hearts and damaged emotions. Had our wounds been ones that could be seen with the eye, such as a cut or a broken bone, we would have known what to do to facilitate healing. Broken hearts and emotional wounds are often left for time to heal, simply because we don't know that God wants to heal our emotional hurt, too.

Part of recovery is to face the truth of our lives, whether it is wrongs we have committed or wrongs done to us. It is this truth, along with the truth of *God's Word*, that sets us free. Yes, this is usually very painful, but this is a healing pain. As we see the hurts, we can bring them to Jesus, who will gently clean and wash those wounds so that healing can take place. No wound is too grave nor is any scratch so minor that he isn't concerned. Today, bring that broken heart to him, knowing that as that deep emotional wounding is touched by him, recovery and wholeness become more and more obvious.

Lord, I bring all the brokenness in my life to you for healing.

Psalm
148

*Praise the Lord. Praise the Lord from the
heavens, praise him in the heights above.
(v. 1)*

Praise the Lord! He has given us at least one
hundred forty-eight days of sobriety. He has
reached into the deepest pit and brought us into
a land of hope and light. He has walked with us
in the sunlight of recovery and the darkness of
discouragement. He has carried us when we
could not walk, and he has encouraged us when
our steps faltered. Our God has given us his healing Word for our diseased bodies, souls, and spirits—and recovery drives out the sickness. If God
has given us one hundred forty-eight days in recovery, then we can trust that he will not abandon
us—he will continue to walk with us.

Praise the Lord for hope, help, healing, and
hearing us when we cry out. Praise him for love,
grace, and mercy. Praise him for the journey of
recovery—praise him for our own personal songs
of recovery. Praise him!

*Lord, I praise you for another day of sober
living—your gift to me.*

Psalm
149

*For the Lord takes delight in his people; he
crowns the humble with salvation. (v. 4)*

The Lord delights in his people. Could that be
true? God delights in each one of us whether we
deserve it in our own estimation or not. God
places a high value upon us. We would go to the
ends of the earth to have a person's approval, to
know that someone special thought well of us. We
work extra hours and go miles out of our way to
do something nice for someone because we want
to feel good about ourselves. The God of this universe, the King of Kings, thinks we are a delight.
Mothers and fathers look at their little baby: no
hair, wrinkled skin, no control over muscles, blad-
der, or bowels. This child is theirs, and although
he or she can give nothing, do nothing, and has
accomplished not one thing, those parents love
their child just because the child *is*. As those parents love that child, our Father loves us, delights
in us, and wants to bless our lives with salvation
from our addiction/codependency. He crowns us
with the gift of recovery.

*O God, thank you for your opinion about me—
even when I don't measure up to it.*

Psalm
150

Let everything that has breath praise the Lord.
Praise the Lord. (v. 6)

One hundred fifty days of recovery! Maybe a few months ago, as we began this journey, we were not sure we would get past the "getting clean" stage of recovery. We lived through that, and then came the pain of staying clean on difficult days. God was faithful to us on those difficult days. As we have faithfully worked the Twelve Steps—over and over—our spiritual, emotional, and physical well-being has strengthened. Now, months into recovery, we know that recovery is a life-style to maintain rather than a goal to be reached. We have come to know that our powerlessness is a blessing that helped us turn our lives and wills over to God. This gave us courage to take a moral inventory and share it. Next came removal of defects of character and shortcomings. Then the continuing growth of recovery began, building on the foundation: ongoing inventories, improving conscious contact with God, and sharing our stories of recovery with others. This has worked for hundreds of thousands of people, and it will work for us.

Praise God, who is the author of recovery!

Lord, I thank you for men and women who
are living Testimonies that I can make recovery
my life-style.